Keys
FREEDOM

Keys
to emotional
FREEDOM

Unlocking the Doors of
Your Heart and Mind

Robin Martens

If the Son sets you free, you will be free indeed.
—John 8:36, NIV

Beacon Hill Press of Kansas City
Kansas City, Missouri

Copyright 2004
by Robin Martens and Beacon Hill Press of Kansas City

ISBN 083-412-1743

Printed in the
United States of America

Cover Design: Darlene Filley

Library of Congress Cataloging-in-Publication Data

Martens, Robin, 1955-
   Keys to emotional freedom : unlocking the doors of your heart and mind / [Robin Martens].
      p. cm.
   Includes bibliographical references.
   ISBN 0-8341-2174-3 (pbk.)
   1. Emotions—Religious aspects—Christianity. 2. Mental health—Religious aspects—Christianity. I. Title.

   BV4597 .3.M37 2004
   248.4—dc22

                                                                    2004022201

10   9   8   7   6   5   4   3   2   1

Contents

Acknowledgments

Thanks to friends who encouraged me along the way, clients who shared their hearts, mentors who lit the path, and my friends at Beacon Hill Press of Kansas City for their dedication to share God's love through the written word.

Special thanks to my family—the stars in my sky; to my husband, Gene, for his love, patience, and support; to our daughter, Mary, and her husband, Luke, for their artistic passion and support for my dreams; to our son, Stephen, and his wife, Jessica, for their unflagging faith and encouragement; and to my parents, Pastor Al and Lee Runge, for teaching me to trust God always.

Foreword

The author of this book is my personal friend. At various times we've worked together exploring the subject of unfinished emotional business, burdens, unhealed wounds, and what to do with them. In doing this, we've learned firsthand how awesome and real God's presence and faithfulness are.

What about you? Do you know how real and faithful He is? If you don't, this book can help you. You'll notice that the author always directs you to God. That's because your burdens and mine are not *our* business—they're God's business.

Our Creator didn't design us humans to carry burdens. We're not pack animals. We're made to abide in the presence of the living God, living in covenant with Him, depending on and interacting with Him about *everything*. That's why He tells us to cast all of our cares upon Him, for He deeply cares for us and holds us always in the most tender regard (see 1 Pet. 5:5-7).

Robin Martens directs you right to the ultimate Source of all good things in this book. What bothers you? What fills you with shame? What do you lack? What do you crave and lust after? What hurts and drives you into fear or obsession? Whatever it is, you don't need to try handling it alone. Nor should you depend on others who are as empty and limited as you are.

Go to Him and enter into His eternal, transforming presence. Bring Him your hurts, horrors, humiliations, hatreds, and ravishing, unsatisfied hungers and unfinished business. Lay it all before Him and see what He'll do.

—*John Marquez*
Director of Christ-Life Ministries

Introduction

Many of us live with heavy burdens, limping through life with little enjoyment. Depression is commonplace and life is difficult. Learning to effectively release our burdens to God can bring joy into our lives.

Daily we're tripped up by obstacles, slammed by harsh reality, and threatened by potential disaster. The Bible guarantees that we'll face trouble, but it also promises overwhelming power and enduring joy.

As a Christian counselor, I've guided hundreds of persons along the path to emotional freedom. Over the years I've observed that keys to this freedom are often overlooked by the freedom-seekers themselves. Many sincere seekers try to apply truth and are disappointed when their emotions aren't healed. Scriptural truths are recognized, applied, and processed in their minds rather than in their hearts.

In order to allow God's truth to renew us, our hearts must be as open to Him as our minds are. As the Creator invades and restores each area of our emotional realm, our hearts begin to mend.

If you've prayed earnestly about an emotional or relationship struggle and seen little progress, this book may be just what you need. It contains simple yet crucial scriptural keys that will allow God to help you. Don't let the simplicity of these principles fool you into thinking they don't contain great spiritual power. God loves you too much to make the path to wholeness complicated.

It's true that there may be pain involved in bringing your hurts to God for healing. But as you trust Him, He'll carry you through to emotional freedom.

Getting free is habit—a new life skill. Key truths that you'll learn in this book are applied in different ways throughout. One key to freedom is to apply truth in all-encompassing ways rather than to just one area of your life.

This book is not a substitute for professional help, and I encourage you to be open to the path God has for you. He often heals through physicians and Christian counselors, and it's wise to seek support from friends and professionals when you feel overwhelmed. Don't attempt to cope with severe emotional and spiritual problems on your own.

Most of my clients have recovered without medication or hospitalization, but sometimes they've needed anti-depressants or interventions, because they weren't able to function or were in danger of self-harm. Medications for depression, anxiety, and other emotional struggles are sometimes necessary, beneficial, and even life-saving. There should be no shame in taking insulin to manage diabetes or in taking medication to overcome depression.

All medications, including those for emotional distress, have the potential of unpleasant side-effects and should not be used unless truly necessary. Also, medication can sometimes mask symptoms. It's better to learn skills to overcome emotional difficulties. But in the case of severe emotional distress, thank God for the safety net of doctors, hospitals, and medications. A doctor or psychiatrist who specializes in mental health should be the one to prescribe medication for emotional problems if needed.

The more trustworthy supports you have, the better. "Where there is no counsel, purposes are frustrated, but with many counselors they are accomplished" (Prov. 15:22). Ask God to help you find trustworthy friends and professionals if you don't have a support system in place.

Much healing is to be found in a caring relationship with a wise friend. It's important that you find safe people who accept you and will guide you toward the Father. Often wounded people either will not trust at all or tend to trust too quickly. Be careful in determining whom to trust, and take each relationship slowly.

"Confess to one another therefore your faults (your slips, your false steps, your offenses, your sins) and pray [also] for one another, that you may be healed and restored [to a spiritual tone of mind and heart]. The earnest (heartfelt, continued) prayer of a righteous man makes tremendous power available [dynamic in its working]" (James 5:16).

It's important to get a complete physical exam to rule out possible contributing factors such as head injury, chemical imbalance, illness, or even allergies that may cause emotional distress. In this book I will discuss primarily the emotional and spiritual dimensions rather than physical problems.

Pray for God's guidance when you work on emotional healing, remembering that emotions and spirituality are closely connected. You can take your burdens to the all-powerful, all-knowing God.

I invite you on this journey into the emotional realm.

The names and details of the examples used in this book have been changed to protect the confidentiality of my clients.

PART I

Keys to Freedom from Emotional Bondage

Carry Me, Lord

When you're burdened down with care
And there is no relief,
Lift up your head and say this prayer:
O Lord, won't You carry me?

Carry me; carry me—
On wings of angels set me free.
Joy returns when You come to me,
O Lord, when You carry me.

My spirit's weighed down,
And I want to be free.
On wings of angels set me free.
Till my blinded eyes will see

Only You will carry me.
O Lord, You carry me.
My spirit's laid low,
And I want to be free.

O Lord, You carry me.
It's You who carries me.
Carry me over the stormy sea.
O Lord, You carry me.

You carried my sorrows upon that tree,
And I know You'll carry me.
You purchased my freedom at Calvary
And I know You carry me.

Lift me up and carry me
Through this life till all can see
It's You who carry me.
O Lord, You carry me.

—Robin Martens

1

Confess
Heart Honesty

"I don't want to be here, but I need help." Sarah's face flushed as she looked up.

"What makes you say that?"

"I always thought seeing a counselor was for people with serious problems, not for me. But lately I've thought of suicide a lot."

Thunder rumbled in the distance. Sarah's hair was soaked from her dash to the reception door from her red Toyota. Her chart said she was 35, but she looked younger. Her black sweater reflected her mood.

Sarah proceeded to tell me about her life. She was raised in a Christian home but felt her parents' rules were restrictive. Her dad never showed much affection. In college she enjoyed partying, but one night she barely escaped being raped and decided to stop drinking. She rededicated her life to God when she was 21.

Sarah often clashed with her perfectionist husband, Mike. She wanted to relax and enjoy life, but Mike's standards were demanding. She realized she wasn't emotionally available for her five-year-old daughter, Megan. Depression weighed her down almost constantly.

I probed to find the cause of her depression. Sarah was only slightly overweight, but she was miserable about it and obsessed about diets. She felt her in-laws didn't approve of her. Sometimes she wondered if God or her husband loved her. Sarah couldn't identify a major stressor causing her depression but felt it was caused by many disappointments that had built up over time. Life just wasn't the way she wanted it to be.

Sarah had felt depressed off and on in her earlier years, but for almost a year now the sadness was "unbearable at times."

I wasn't surprised that she had suffered for nearly a year before making an appointment. Counseling is often a last resort. "How have you tried to relieve your depression?" I asked.

"We go to church regularly, and my faith helps. I keep praying God will make the depression go away. I think He's helped some, but I keep getting depressed. I don't understand it. I try to stay busy so I won't think about being sad, but lately nothing is working."

As I ended our counseling session, hail was pounding the roof. I referred Sarah to a doctor who could evaluate if an antidepressant was necessary, and I had her sign a contract promising not to hurt herself. For homework, I encouraged her to journal what her feelings would say if they could talk.

The next Tuesday Sarah was late for her appointment.

"I tried journaling, but I couldn't do it," she said.

"What was difficult about it?"

"I don't like to think about what I'm feeling, so it was hard to write anything down. All I wanted to do was swear and complain. Why would it help to write that stuff out? I'm disgusted with myself, and I'm sure God is disgusted with me too."

"Sarah, God already knows how you feel. His flashlight shines straight into the darkest, most damaged part of your heart. He loves each part of your broken heart. He wants to clean out the poison of old hurts so your heart can mend. When you bring your despairing places to Him, then His light and love brings healing. Being honest with God doesn't mean you're trying to justify a bad attitude. Emotional honesty is admitting that you can't heal your hurts alone."

I explained to Sarah that we tend to make emotional recovery more complicated than it needs to be. In fact, little children are experts at healing emotionally.

Children are emotionally honest. Their hearts don't know how to be dishonest. Children feel, say, and show their emotions. They don't fight their feelings—they flow with them, release them, and return to joy. When a child's emotions erupt, it isn't always pretty, but it's always honest. Children innately know how to release emotion.

I asked Sarah how her daughter Megan handled emotions when she was two or three years old.

Sarah smiled. "Megan used to fall apart whenever she was upset or tired. She screamed, cried, and was an angry mess. But a few minutes after she calmed down, or after she had a nap, she loved everyone and everything again."

I told Sarah, "Little children are a perfect example of the system God put inside each of us to help us release negative emotions and return to peace and joy. Children are honest about what they feel, and they follow their hearts."

As we mature, we need to learn more appropriate ways to control and also release feelings. However, sometimes instead of learning emotional skills, we just shut down our emotions. We disconnect our God-given emotional healing system and try to reason everything out instead of following our hearts.

What does it mean to follow your heart? The following verse directs us:

> You shall love the Lord your God with all your heart and with all your soul and with all your mind (intellect). [Deut. 6:5.] This is the great (most important, principal) and first commandment.) And a second is like it: You shall love your neighbor as [you do] yourself. [Lev. 19:18.] These two commandments sum up and upon them depend all the Law and the Prophets (Matt. 22:37-40).

God wants us to love Him with all our hearts. How can we do this if we're unwilling to look honestly at our emotions? To shut down our emotions is to close our hearts to God, to others, even to our own self-awareness. To ignore or deny our own emotions is being hardhearted. When we shut down our negative emotions in order to avoid them, we also suppress love and joy. We barricade the doors to our hearts.

"I will give them an undivided heart and put a new spirit within them; I will remove from them their heart of stone and give them a heart of flesh. Then they will follow my decrees and be careful to keep my laws. They will be my people, and I will be their God" (Ezek. 11:19-20, NIV).

The first key to emotional freedom is to admit
our true emotions and our need for God's help.

Don't Ignore Emotions

God did not give us emotions in order to annoy, burden, or destroy us. Emotions are a tremendous gift—if we keep them healthy.

"I am the LORD your God, who teaches you what is best for you, who directs you in the way you should go. If only you had paid attention to my commands, your peace would have been like a river, your righteousness like the waves of the sea" (Isa. 48:17-18, NIV).

We can be *careful* with emotions without ignoring them. Our emotions are meant to be a valuable compass in determining our path. Peace and joy can be signals to go forward. Distress can be a warning to stop or retreat.

Just as nerve endings warn of physical damage, painful emotions warn of heart damage. Our negative emotions can be compared to the warning lights on the dashboard of a car. It wouldn't be wise to disconnect the wires under the dashboard because the warning lights are annoying. Similarly, we can get ourselves into serious trouble if we ignore—or disconnect—our emotions.

"Motion" is part of the word "emotion," which is from the *Latin word *movere,* meaning "to move."[1] Emotional reactions can be stored in our minds or released when the situation is over. To find emotional freedom, the negative emotions must be released—but only in healthful ways.

Emotions may be hard to face, especially when they gather force. Handling emotions can compare to operating a pressure cooker. When the safety valve is opened, steam escapes with no problem. Close the valve, and rising heat explodes the lid and contents, creating a mess. Emotional explosions create damage, but we can maintain control if we keep the safety valve open by accepting and honestly expressing our emotions in safe ways.

Find a Balance

In my first few years as a counselor, I helped clients improve their thought patterns by challenging negative thinking and replacing it with positive truths. Practicing positive thinking was helpful, but it didn't seem to root out deep-seated burdens, repetitive struggles, or strongholds.

In order to get longstanding emotional problems to heal, each client had to be honest about heart struggles.

Emotional freedom requires a balance—to be positive in our outlook and emotionally honest about hurts, fears, and irritations at the same time.

It's wise to choose a positive focus by dwelling on God, His Word, and the wonderful aspects of life. However, if we ignore emotional wounds that need healing, we're in trouble. We can't get free by trying to clean up our acts by ourselves and pretending we don't feel what we feel.

Truth includes our reality; lies deny reality. If we lie to ourselves and cut off our emotions by our own efforts, our burdens will grow heavier. But if we walk in faith and emotional honesty and bring our emotions to God for healing, we'll walk in light and freedom.

Acknowledge Emotions Without Allowing Them to Rule

Parents experience the force of their child's emotions from the first wail of protest to independent, adolescent stubbornness. A child's emotions can be inconvenient, embarrassing, and even heartbreaking. So we teach our children self-restraint. Balanced self-control is a virtue. Uncontrolled emotions destroy relationships, careers, and reputations.

"The fruit of the Spirit is . . . self-control" (Gal. 5:23, NIV)

We discussed the value of proper control of emotions. Sarah told me sometimes she shared too much too quickly with people she just met. She admitted she leaned too hard on others in hopes they would make her feel better. Her emotional transparency didn't seem to help her heal or develop relationships. In fact, it seemed to scare people away.

Self-control is important in this journey to freedom. But *excessive* control of emotions results in a joyless, cold, emotionless existence. We should strive for balance, avoiding out-of-control emotion as well as becoming emotionally frozen.

Emotions can be managed well with God's help. Although it's wise to uncover our emotional reality, we must be careful to not harm, overburden, or threaten others in the process. Often our emotions need only to be vented to God. If you share with others, be sure they're trustworthy. It's wise to seek help when needed *and* use discretion.

As we begin to heal emotionally, it may feel as if we're headed in the wrong direction. Guilt and confusion and fears assault us, and an inner voice may tell us to turn back. Ignore these false warnings, and walk through the intense emotion while holding on to God's hand. Eventually we'll find ourselves on the other side of the dark tunnel, free from that stronghold. Then we can say, "That wasn't so bad. I wish I had walked out of that problem years ago!"

If you can't control your behavior while processing emotions, then wait until God enables you to grow in self-discipline. If your emotional struggles are intense, chronic, or extremely painful, find a godly counselor to support you. The more positive supports you have, the better.

Remember: strong emotions should not be used as an excuse for wrong behavior or bad choices.

"Not Me"

Sarah stomped in for our third appointment and flung her coat at the chair. I thought she might be upset with me, but then she blurted out, "I'd like to slap Wendy. She's a lady at my church who thinks she's something special. But I'd never really hit someone. That's not me."

"Who's feeling the anger if it isn't you?" I asked.

Sarah had to admit she was angry before she could make progress.

"Out of the abundance (overflow) of the heart his mouth speaks" (Luke 6:45).

Often when a depressed person experiences anger, it's a sign that his or her frozen emotions are thawing. It's possible to be angry in a healthy way, but first we have to take responsibility for what we're feeling.

Sarah didn't *want* to be angry with anyone. So instead of finding a proper vent for her anger, she pushed it down inside. The anger banged painfully against the closed doors of her heart and contributed to her depression.

Sincere people often don't realize what's going on in their own hearts, because they think it's wrong to *examine* their emotions.

"Search me, O God, and know my heart; test me and know my anxious thoughts. See if there is any offensive way in me, and lead me in the way everlasting" (Ps. 139:23-24, NIV).

Just as a reporter may first discuss a devastating earthquake and then a horrific crime and finally, minutes later, joke about the weather, we can become dissociated from our emotions. If we don't know what we feel, how can we ask for help? How can we get free if we won't admit that we're bound?

Being honest with God, with trustworthy friends, and with ourselves reveals to us the roadblocks in our hearts. When we see the roadblocks, we can allow God to remove them. Don't deny your emotions. Emotional and spiritual healing is not obtained by cutting off emotions. This doesn't apply to *passing* negative feelings, which should be released before they become lodged in our hearts. But if hurts stick and fester, they must be examined in order to heal.

Ask God for His assistance, and pour your fear, sadness, or rage out to Him. We have nothing to fear when we come to God for help. Healing and spiritual maturity are gained by bringing our reality to God. He's a loving father who desires wholeness for His children. Denial stalls recovery; the truth sets us free.

Have We Forgotten About the Heart?

"All the ways of a man are pure in his own eyes, but the Lord weighs the spirits (the thoughts and intents of the heart)" (Prov. 16:2).

"We have the prophetic word [made] firmer still. You will do well to pay close attention to it as to a lamp shining in a dismal (squalid and dark) place, until the day breaks through [the gloom] and the Morning Star rises (comes into being) in your hearts" (2 Pet. 1:19).

Sarah never knew her father's love, and she fought with insecurity. She asked me, "How can I be OK when even my own father and my in-laws reject me?" She lacked confidence to succeed.

Her pastor preached God's love every Sunday, but it never *felt* real to her. The truth of God's love never traveled from her head to her heart.

The heart is "thought of as the vital center of one's being, emotions and sensibilities; the seat or repository of emotions."[2]

The word "heart" is overused. We tend to think of the heart in sentimental terms and associate it with romance and flowers. We "love" others from our hearts.

But it's also our hearts speaking when we rage. Our hearts may overflow with fear, depression, or anger. We're emotional beings. Our thoughts and motives can be calm and rational, or they can be fueled by emotions that are conceived in our hearts. It seems we forget or don't realize we need to apply God's truth to emotions.

To confess our heart truths, we need to bring *all* emotions to God. If we humble ourselves and confess 100 percent of the pain, anger, lust, bitterness, or fears, He's able to invade that area of the heart with His love and healing.

Often we pray from our intellect with open minds. But our hearts aren't open to God. God will bring progressive healing as He is invited into each part of the emotional realm.

Sarah talked in a circular pattern about her past hurts. When someone continually rehashes problems in the same way, it's a sign he or she is stuck. Instead of processing the painful emotions out of his or her system so healing can begin, the person tries to intellectually solve the problems.

Our reality is comprised of spiritual, physical, intellectual, and emotional facets. We can't heal emotional hurts the same way we solve intellectual problems or the same way our bodies heal. I once heard John Marquez say, "Imagine your life is like a house with different floors, with your spiritual, intellectual, emotional, and physical dimensions represented by each level. If a fire is raging on the emotional floor, but you pour water only onto the intellectual and spiritual floor, then you're not getting to the cause of the fire."[3]

Our bodies heal according to physical principles. Our minds resolve problems by thinking them through or by weighing pros and cons. An important key to emotional healing is to realize that emotions can't be solved like math problems. Negative emotions must be released for us to heal. However, we can't release emotions unless we first admit they're there.

We can release emotions by venting or crying in healthful ways. If we rage at our families, we may feel relief, but the hurt and anger can boomerang on us. If we vent by journaling, praying, or talking to a trusted friend or counselor, then no one will get hurt. If when we cry we berate ourselves and hate ourselves, we wound ourselves more. But if we cry and simply release the emotion as a small child would—without analyzing or judging—the emotion is released, and joy can return.

We all wrestle with heart wounds that need to be cleansed and healed. You're not alone; everyone's heart breaks. Don't be ashamed to admit to God when you're hurt, afraid, or angry.

Of course, it makes sense to avoid evil, distressing or painful emotions. Often, we just don't need to go there. However, we may have ingrained patterns of painful emotions that don't go away when we ignore them.

Sarah started journaling her feelings about her relationships with her father, her in-laws, and God. I told her to write on cheap spiral notebook paper and to tear up anything she wouldn't want others to see. The purpose of journaling is to cleanse the heart, not to damage relationships. Sarah let her anger, despair, and sorrow speak without censoring what she felt. She brought her feelings into God's healing light and allowed Him to clean out pain. She wrote letters she didn't send, expressing her pain to those who had hurt her.

Sarah started to realize God is not like her father or any other human. God's love is constant.

It's been said that life's battles are won or lost in our minds, and that's true. But life's battles are also won or lost in our hearts. Our hearts hold keys to victory we often miss. God will fight and win battles for us when we fully commit our minds and *hearts* to Him.

Our struggles are not with calm, objective thoughts; our struggles are with subjective, emotional thoughts. The extreme emotions of our hearts can push us into behavior our rational minds would not condone.

The Bible refers to our hearts more frequently than to our minds. Concordances list the word "heart" more than twice as often as "mind." How can we not apply God's principles to emotions when so many scriptural directives concern our hearts?

"This people's *heart* has become calloused. . . . Otherwise they might see with their eyes, hear with their ears, understand with their *hearts* and turn, and I would heal them" (Matt. 13:15, NIV, emphasis added).

Don't Fear Emotions

"True (genuine) worshipers will worship the Father in spirit and in truth (reality); for the Father is seeking just such people as these as His worshipers" (John 4:23).

God wants us to be honest with Him even when it hurts.

We're often overloaded with busy schedules and information coming at us through television, radio, and the mail. We can become so distracted that we fail to stay in touch with our hearts. We spend too much of our energy ignoring our emotions rather than dealing with them in a beneficial way.

The most common way to deal with negative emotions is to try to keep a positive attitude and hold the negative feelings at arm's length. People who deal with their emotions this way may end up in a counselor's office trying to control the overflow.

Sarah isn't the only person who has had a hard time understanding how to release negative emotions in order to become free.

It may be hard to find a safe environment in which to air your emotions. Work conversations avoid religion, politics, and other emotional topics. Dinner discussions condense the day's events. Church prayers request healing for cancer or heart disease, not depression or rage.

How can we find the answers if we can't ask the questions?

How can we feel loved by our families if we've closed ourselves off from them emotionally?

People often leave the Sunday morning service with the same anxiety, sadness, and anger they came with. The hurts, fears, and addictions we fail to bring to the light gather power in darkness and may overwhelm us.

"If we [really] are living and walking in the Light, as He [himself] is in the Light, we have [true, unbroken] fellowship with one another, and the blood of Jesus Christ His Son cleanses (removes) us from all sin and guilt [keeps us cleansed from sin in all its forms and manifestations]" (1 John 1:7).

With our Heavenly Father, there is no condemnation, only forgiveness and restoration. God is waiting until He can pour His compassion on us (Isa. 30:18). It doesn't make God angry when we admit our true thoughts and feelings. He is aware of everything within our hearts, and He's glad when we're finally honest with Him.

What's in your heart?

Which emotions cause you to struggle?

Would you like help?

Progressive and powerful healing is available as we open our hearts and submit to God's working in us, rather than trying to contain our emotions. As God removes the sludge suffocating our lives, not only do we heal, but we're also able to grow.

Sometimes the process of releasing impacted, festering, old emotional build-up is too painful on our own. Although God is the only one who can heal us, sometimes we need a friend to support us along the way. More support is needed for chronic or severe emotional distress, and it's beneficial to seek aid from as many sources as possible, such as mature and compassionate Christian friends, family members, counselors, support groups, pastors, or church workers.

As you go through the following checklist, rate the intensity of your emotional patterns from 1 to 10. The intensity indicates how much pain you carry around with you. Any recurring emotion stronger than a 5 needs healing, and emotional patterns that consistently register close to 10 require professional help. If your emotional pattern is extreme and interfering with your ability to function, to seek assistance from a Christian counselor or physician. God often provides support and healing through counseling or medical care.

God wants to heal you. The first step is openhearted confession that includes your emotions—not just your intellect. Confession means total honesty.

Checklist to Identify Heart Truths

1. Do you experience a recurring pattern of painful or difficult emotions?
2. Do you have emotions you keep trying to avoid that threaten to spill into your life?
3. Do you have a pattern of feeling rejected or lonely?
4. What irritates you more than you think it should?
5. What fills you with guilt or shame?
6. What do you feel you lack? What do you crave or lust after?
7. What hurts and pushes you toward fear or obsession?
8. How long have these patterns continued? When did they start?
9. Do you feel God is distant and uncaring when you experience these emotions?
10. Are you able to pray when in the midst of these emotions?
11. Are you uncomfortable being alone in quiet and uneasy with what may overflow from your heart?
12. With God's direction, are you willing to explore, feel, and confess recurring emotional patterns rather than analyze them?

Prayer to Confess Heart Truths

Father God, thank You for Your kindness and mercy. Thank You for being close to the brokenhearted [Ps. 34:18]. *Thank You for wanting to cleanse my hurts and heal me. In 1 John 1:9 Your Word says that if we confess our faults, You are faithful and just to forgive us and cleanse us from all unrighteousness. You promise not to reject or condemn us when we come to You in truth. You only forgive and heal.*

I admit to You the truth in my heart. I lay open before You my struggle with _____ [depression, envy, bitterness, irritation, anger, anxiety, lust, or any other emotion]. *Forgive me for not opening this place in my heart to You before. I ask You to be in charge of these conflicts within me. I trust in Your kindness and mercy. In Jesus name I pray. Amen.*

"The LORD is close to the brokenhearted and saves those who are crushed in spirit" (Ps. 34:18, NIV).

2

Believe

God's Power Will Rescue You

Gusts of wind whipped through the trees and sent leaves dancing across the parking lot. I leaned my elbow on my oak rolltop desk as I listened.

Sarah sat on the couch across from me with red-rimmed eyes. "I didn't realize how much pain I had. Some areas are healing, but more pain is surfacing, and it seems like a confused mess. I don't know where all these feelings are coming from."

I handed her the box of tissues and assured her, "You don't need to know the exact memories they come from—all you need to do is release them. God will take care of the rest."

"But how do I know that? It seems that I should figure out what I'm feeling, not just release my emotions into thin air."

I explained to Sarah that our emotions heal when we simply release them, not when we figure them out. We heal emotionally by *letting go* of painful feelings. In Scripture it's described as giving our burdens to God.

Just as our bodies heal when the virus, infection, or cancer is removed, our emotions heal when the hurt, irritation, bitterness, or fear is released. We figure out and resolve math problems, but our intellect doesn't resolve or heal emotions. In fact, trying to figure out emotions can prevent or slow the healing process. We can't release our hurts when we're busy analyzing them.

Sarah's expression was puzzled. "It's hard to believe God can help me with the depression I struggled with for so long. If He can help me, why hasn't He done something before?"

"Sarah, you can trust God more than you trust your own history. Maybe you never trusted God enough to open the floodgates of your emotions."

The only way to walk through the door to freedom is to let God carry us. Confessing to God how we feel isn't enough to find emotional healing. The second step is to believe in God's healing power, pour out our hearts, and wait for Him to rescue us.

Emotional healing isn't complicated, but neither is it easy. In order to relax our guard, feel, and release pain, we have to believe God will carry us through it. We open our hearts only to those we trust. If we don't trust someone, our spirit closes to him or her. We don't want the person to do anything for us. In fact, we want to stay as far away as possible. Likewise, if we don't trust God, we won't allow Him to carry us.

Thin air won't hold you up, but a powerful airplane will. Trust in yourself is as limited as you are, but when you trust in God's limitless power, He'll carry you through all of life's storms. "Lean on, trust in, and be confident in the Lord with all your heart and mind and do not rely on your own insight or understanding. In all your ways know, recognize, and acknowledge Him, and He will direct and make straight and plain your paths" (Prov. 3:5-6).

The second key to emotional freedom is to believe and trust God enough to relax and release damaged emotions.

Daddy, God

"Listen to me . . . you whom I have upheld since you were conceived, and have carried since your birth. Even to your old age and gray hairs I am he, I am he who will sustain you. I have made you and I will carry you; I will sustain you and I will rescue you" (Isa. 46:3-4, NIV).

Were you fortunate enough to have a daddy when you were small? Not just a father, not just a dad, but a *daddy*—someone big enough to heal your hurts, fix your toys, and be there when you needed him. If not, I have good news for you: you can have a daddy now.

Nothing is too hard for the One who created the universe. Bring all your troubles to Him. God loved you when you were created in the womb and when you were born, and He still loves you.

"You did form my inward parts; You did knit me together in my mother's womb" (Ps. 139:13).

What do you think it takes to achieve escape velocity? To lift us out of complacency, boredom, depression, anxiety or failure takes a higher power—God's power.

We break out of earth's downward pull through childlike trust. Scripture offers the role model of a little child to light our path (Matt. 18:1-4). Little children trust someone bigger to care for and carry them. The journey to emotional freedom starts with childlike trust.

Childish faults such as foolishness, ignorance, and impulsiveness are not desirable. But God highly prizes childlike virtues— honesty, open hearts, and trust.

Even when we physically mature, we're still children in relationship with God. The emotional and spiritual realms of our lives work on different principles than our physical maturation. In fact, our maturity increases in direct proportion to how much we depend on God.

An attitude of total reliance on God wields power, but it wars against our independence. You may say, "Don't we mature? Can't we learn to walk in cooperation with God?"

Yes, we can, but it isn't exactly an equal relationship. It's not like walking with your spouse or your friend.

Acts 17:28 says, "In him we live and move and have our being." God grips our atoms and molecules so we won't dissipate into nothingness. We're dependent on Him for our very breath. God flung the stars into space and fills the universe; we're powerless compared to Him. Yet He stoops to regard us with love and longs for us to let Him help. Although God holds us together, He won't rescue us from our self-sufficiency until we let Him.

Usually the only time we let someone else take over is when we reach the end of our own resources. We can persist until life pounds us into the dust, but is that wise? We can struggle along, or we can admit we need assistance. We don't have to wait until life smashes us.

Turning Point

The powerful first two steps of Alcoholics Anonymous parallel scriptural principles. Lives change as these truths are applied.

The first step is to hit bottom and realize our lives have become unmanageable and that we're helpless to correct the situation. The second step is to realize that a power greater than ourselves can restore our lives to sanity.[1]

These two steps echo this Bible passage: "Since we've compiled this long and sorry record as sinners (both us and them) and proved that we are utterly incapable of living the glorious lives God wills for us, God did it for us. Out of sheer generosity he put us in right standing with himself. A pure gift. He got us out of the mess we're in and restored us to where he always wanted us to be. And he did it by means of Jesus Christ" (Rom. 3:23-24, TM). God is the only higher power who loves us.

Problems turn around when we stop struggling and let God take over. He'll carry us only after we give up. The more quickly we hit bottom with our problem, the sooner we escape. We don't have to be a miserable wreck before we admit we can't do it on our own! We can choose our turning point.

A. W. Tozer said it this way: "The reason why many are still troubled, still seeking, still making little forward progress is because they haven't yet come to the end of themselves. We're still trying to give orders, and interfering with God's work within us."[2]

The God who created you wants to carry you—if you're humble enough to let Him. "Blessed be the Lord, Who bears our burdens and carries us day by day, even the God Who is our salvation! Selah (pause, and calmly think of that)!" (Ps. 68:19). "Salvation" in this verse is the Hebrew word *yeshuwah*—"something *saved . . .* that is, *deliverance*; hence *aid, victory, prosperity*: deliverance, health, help (-ing), salvation, save, saving (health), welfare."[3]

We can trust God only when we know His love, but it's a struggle to understand our Heavenly Father's love. God's love is as high above our understanding as the stars are above the earth. We see only a glimmer of His love in those around us. But His love is limitless, and His love can be trusted.

A loving father desires to help his children, especially when they suffer or struggle. God is your loving Father, and His compassion reaches out to you in the midst of your emotional storms.

When we're smashed by life, we can wonder, "Where is God? Has He abandoned me?"

No, He has not abandoned you. He's still here. He's with every believing heart. Through every trial and distress, He's the one who never changes and never forsakes His own. It doesn't matter how dark the day—His light still shines on us.

The Kingdom Messenger

Sabbath arrived on a sultry summer day in Nazareth. Outside, a gentle breeze provided little relief to the worshipers inside. On the synagogue's right side, somber young men in black skullcaps stared straight ahead as silver-haired men nodded and slept. Sunlight filtered through columns and shone on the men. On the left, mothers soothed their babies. A few girls suppressed giggles. Women glanced at the girls and frowned.

A local carpenter, Jesus, stepped forward to read the Torah: "The Spirit of the Lord is on me, because he has anointed me to preach good news to the poor. He has sent me to proclaim freedom for the prisoners, and recovery of sight to the blind, to release the oppressed, to proclaim the year of the Lord's favor."

Jesus asserted, "Today this scripture is fulfilled in your hearing (Luke 4:18-19, 21, NIV).

Amazed at His words, then enraged when He refused to perform a miracle for them, the crowd shoved Jesus out of the synagogue toward a nearby cliff to throw Him over. He calmly passed through their midst to safety.

Jesus performed the greatest miracle when He died on a cross and paid the price for our healing. "He was despised and rejected by men, a man of sorrows, and familiar with suffering. Like one from whom men hide their faces he was despised, and we esteemed him not. Surely he took up our infirmities and carried our sorrows, yet we considered him stricken by God, smitten by him, and afflicted. But he was pierced for our transgressions, he was crushed for our iniquities; the punishment that brought us peace was upon him, and by his wounds we are healed" (Isa. 53:3-5, NIV).

The stunning news of the gospel applies to our emotions as well as our spirits. What is the gospel? It's great news! On the

Cross Jesus carried our sorrows and paid the price for our emotional healing as well as for our sins. All we need to do is accept Him and what He's done for us—by His wounds we are healed.

Since Jesus gave His life for our welfare, He can be trusted. Jesus is the opposite of an abuser. Neglectful or abusive people demand their own way. Anyone who went so far as to die to help us cannot be cruel or unreliable.

Jesus' mission was to preach the gospel, mend broken hearts, set captives free, and heal the sick. Jesus' purpose was to demonstrate the love of God.

God sent His Son to deliver us completely. Is it God's will to comfort us and heal our emotions? Yes! To give us light and understanding? Yes! To carry us and our sorrows? Yes, yes, yes!

Even when problems are chronic or extreme, it's never too late to call for help. Even when all hope is gone, it's never too late. Faith can open a door to the miraculous.

Our Comforter

Before Jesus left, He reassured us, "It is profitable (good, expedient, advantageous) for you that I go away. Because if I do not go away, the Comforter (Counselor, Helper, Advocate, Intercessor, Strengthener, Standby) will not come to you [into close fellowship with you]; but if I go away, I will send Him to you [to be in close fellowship with you]" (John 16:7).

The Holy Spirit—the third person of the Trinity, the heavenly Dove, is our comforter. In Zechariah 4:6, God says, "Not by might, nor by power, but by My Spirit" even a mountain will be removed. You have unimaginable power available to carry you with this Friend by your side. He is our resource when all other resources fail us. We're never alone when we have this Comforter.

He's waiting for your invitation.

"All who are led by the Spirit of God are sons of God. For [the Spirit which] you have now received [is] not a spirit of slavery to put you once more in bondage to fear, but you have received the Spirit of adoption [the Spirit producing sonship] in [the bliss of] which we cry, Abba (Father)! Father! The Spirit Himself [thus] testifies together with our own spirit, [assuring us] that we are children of God" (Rom. 8:14-16).

Ministering Angels

"He will command his angels concerning you to guard you in all your ways; they will lift you up in their hands, so that you will not strike your foot against a stone. You will tread upon the lion and the cobra; you will trample the great lion and the serpent" (Ps. 91:11-13, NIV).

Angels are described as "a race of spiritual beings of a nature exalted far above that of man, although infinitely removed from that of God—whose office is 'to do him service in heaven, and by his appointment to succor and defend men on earth.'"[4]

In reference to childlike faith, Jesus says this about us: "Watch that you don't treat a single one of these childlike believers arrogantly. You realize, don't you, that their personal angels are constantly in touch with my Father in heaven?" (Matt. 18:10, TM).

Several years ago our family became entangled in a frightening legal battle. Our well-known lawyer had a reputation for winning court battles, and we depended on his guidance.

I dreamed one night that our lawyer told us he could not work with us any longer. My son and I left his office building wondering what we would do without his help. Outside, an eight-foot-tall man in glowing white walked toward us. On his chest were diamond chariot medals. He took my hand and my son's hand, and we walked together.

A few days later our lawyer called and said he was sorry but that he wasn't able to continue working with us. The news didn't bother us because of my dream—we knew a powerful angel was assigned to our case.

We worked with another lawyer afterward, but our trust was in the Lord. We won the court case, and in every way God vindicated and protected us.

God carries us on the wings of the wind. Thousands of angels wait on His command to minister to us and rescue us. "Bless the LORD, O my soul. O LORD my God, thou art very great; thou art clothed with honour and majesty. Who coverest thyself with light as with a garment; who stretchest out the heavens like a curtain: Who layeth the beams of his chambers in the waters: who maketh the clouds his chariot: who walketh upon the wings of the wind: who maketh his angels spirits; his ministers a flaming fire" (Ps. 104:1-4, KJV).

God's love will carry us, Jesus' sacrifice will rescue us, the Holy Spirit will comfort us, and angels' wings will uplift us. We need only to look up; help is on the way.

Checklist to Identify Beliefs

1. Do you believe you can trust God with all your emotions?
2. Do you struggle with emotions you're afraid or ashamed to bring to God—anger, depression, confusion, anxiety, hatred, or lust?
3. Do you think God will be shocked if you admit your emotions, or do you believe He already sees what's in your heart?
4. Do you feel distant from God? Is there something you need to talk over with Him?
5. Do you think God desires to help you most when you struggle? When do you want to help your children the most?
6. Do you know your crisis points are ideal opportunities to get free?
7. Do you believe honesty includes admitting your emotional struggles?
8. Do you get stressed often? Is there an area in which you could trust God more?
9. Do you feel lonely? Can you open up your loneliness to God?
10. Do you run to God when you feel threatened, or do you handle problems alone?
11. Do you trust God enough to talk to Him about feelings of anger or bitterness?
12. Do you admit the full extent of your emotions, or do you wait until you calm down to pray?

Prayer to Believe God's Rescuing Power

Heavenly Father, forgive me for not trusting You more with my emotions. I put my trust in You as my loving Creator. You know how I'm put together, and You know how I heal.

I place my struggles with _____ into Your capable hands. This is exactly how I feel . . . _____. I ask You to be in charge of this damaged area of my heart. I believe You will heal me. I open my heart to You. Touch me, Lord. I'll stop trying to handle this on my own. Forgive me for getting in Your way in the past. Thank You in advance for helping me. I pray this in Jesus' powerful name. Amen.

3

Accept

Truths to Heal the Heart

———————————

Sarah sat in my office crying. The light from the window shone on her auburn hair. It was silent except for the tick of the clock and her sobbing. Silently I prayed, *Lord I believe You'll set her free.*

Finally Sarah spoke. "It seems as though all my life I've felt sad. I don't even know what's bothering me. I feel miserable today. Even though I've made some progress, I still feel hopeless sometimes."

I asked her, "Have you ever asked Jesus into your depression?"

"What do you mean?"

"When you're depressed, you can open the door to your heart and invite Jesus into the middle of all your sadness and anger."

"I never thought of that. It's hard to pray when I'm depressed."

"Many people say they can't pray when they're struggling, but that's the *best* time to pray. Can I pray with you right now?"

Sarah sighed, "Sure—it couldn't hurt."

"Father God, we praise You for Your love and power. We admit this depression is too big for us, but it's not too big for You. We believe Jesus is Your Son, who came into this world to rescue us and carry our sorrows. We invite You to shine Your light and Your love into Sarah's depression. Jesus, come right into her feelings of hopelessness, and lift these burdens from her. Set her free in Jesus' name."

Sarah was quiet for a moment. "I never prayed that way before." She was calmer and smiled a little.

The third and most important key to emotional
freedom is to accept Jesus' presence directly into
the damaged part of your emotions.

Spiritual Renewal Leads to Emotional Healing

"So then, just as you received Christ Jesus as Lord, continue to live in him" (Col. 2:6, NIV). When we accept Jesus by faith, He rescues us spiritually. However, we need to invite Him into each area of our broken hearts in order to be freed from past and present distress. Jesus is willing to enter into every sorrow, disappointment, and anxiety we experience.

The prerequisite to God healing us is to admit that we can't handle the struggle on our own, believe in His love and power to rescue us, and then accept and wait for His deliverance.

The following passage was written to Christians. Jesus said, "Behold, I stand at the door and knock; if anyone hears and listens to and heeds My voice and opens the door, I will come in to him and will eat with him, and he [will eat] with Me. He who overcomes (is victorious), I will grant him to sit beside Me on My throne, as I Myself overcame (was victorious) and sat down beside My Father on His throne" (Rev. 3:20-21).

This verse refers to our hearts, and the door opens from the inside—the responsibility to open the door is ours. If we want Jesus to enter an area of our lives that has been dark and wounded, we must ask Him. Jesus doesn't force the door open from the outside. He respects our free will and waits until we're ready to trust Him.

We think God will be disappointed if we admit that there's darkness in our hearts, but He's pleased when we're finally honest with Him. We can't cleanse sin from our hearts—only God can do that. We're commanded to admit (confess) to God exactly where we are in our hearts and minds. Then God promises to forgive and heal us (see 1 John 1:9).

Jesus wants to come into our darkness, open the windows,

and bring in light and fresh air. He wants to sit down at our table and eat with us, go to work with us, mediate our arguments, comfort us after nightmares, and live life with us.

Trusting Jesus to deal with us kindly in the dark places of our lives is a key to unlocking the door. God then does the healing work within our hearts.

God knows all about your emotions. Invite Him to carry you through your daily emotional struggles.

We can invite Jesus into traumatic memories, disturbing dreams, and current emotional struggles. Allowing Jesus into our emotions connects our heads to our hearts and connects what we know about God to what we feel. When we allow God to invade our hearts and our emotions of rage, depression, irritability, or anxiety, He brings healing.

Even though we may have a good relationship with God in many ways, struggles may indicate emotional and spiritual doors that we've closed to His love. Each door must be opened by our own will.

The times we feel sad, fearful, obsessed, or angry are the times we need God's help the most. When we struggle with intense emotions, we're often in a dark place where we need God's love and light. Open the shades and unlock the latch. The One who can help you is waiting just outside the door.

Wait upon the Lord

"Those who wait for the Lord [who expect, look for, and hope in Him] shall change and renew their strength and power; they shall lift their wings and mount up [close to God] as eagles [mount up to the sun]; they will run and not be weary, they shall walk and not faint or become tired" (Isa. 40:31).

Sometimes deliverance is instantaneous. Other times we have to wait. Impatience to see results can actually slow the process. When we're impatient we tend to take matters into our own hands. Yes, we need to cooperate with God, but only after we have His direction. God directs us through His Word and through peace. When we wait for God's peace before we act, then we're assured of better outcomes.

The challenge is to keep our hearts open to the Lord. "Submit yourselves, then, to God. Resist the devil, and he will flee from you. Come near to God and he will come near to you" (James 4:7-8, NIV).

As God gradually and lovingly makes you aware of dark rooms in your heart, open each door and invite Jesus in. Admit that you can't handle or resolve the problems on your own. Trust Him to work it out in His way and in His time. Keep trusting and looking for His deliverance. God promises, "You will seek me and find me when you seek me with all your heart" (Jer. 29:13, NIV).

When you pray, wait and hold tightly to God—as you would hold on to a solid rock in a hurricane. This is when powerful breakthroughs occur.

"He arose and rebuked the wind and said to the sea, Hush now! Be still (muzzled)! And the wind ceased [sank to rest as if exhausted by its beating] and there was [immediately] a great calm (a perfect peacefulness)" (Mark 4:39).

God will fight for you. He will calm the storm and carry you on eagles' wings.

"From of old no one has heard nor perceived by the ear, nor has the eye seen a God besides You, Who works and shows Himself active on behalf of him who [earnestly] waits for Him" (Isa. 64:4).

Freedom from Shame

"We do not have a High Priest Who is unable to understand and sympathize and have a shared feeling with our weaknesses and infirmities and liability to the assaults of temptation, but One Who has been tempted in every respect as we are, yet without sinning.

"Let us then fearlessly and confidently and boldly draw near to the throne of grace (the throne of God's unmerited favor to us sinners), that we may receive mercy [for our failures] and find grace to help in good time for every need [appropriate help and well-timed help, coming just when we need it]" (Heb. 4:15-16).

God wants to help with all our struggles. He doesn't want shame to prevent us from coming to Him. Healthy convictions should drive us *to* God, not away from Him. It's healthful to admit when we're wrong and to accept God's forgiveness. It's harmful to allow shame to fester in our souls.

"But I feel ashamed of my behavior, thoughts, and feelings," Sarah said. "I feel inferior to people who seem to have it all together."

I read the following verses to her:

"Therefore [there is] now no condemnation (no adjudging guilty of wrong) for those who are in Christ Jesus, who live [and] walk not after the dictates of the flesh, but after the dictates of the Spirit" (Rom. 8:1).

When we believe in Jesus, accept His gift of rescue, and follow His Spirit, then we're not condemned. When He changes our hearts, we desire to do right, but we still make mistakes. Perfection is not required.

"If we say we have no sin [refusing to admit that we are sinners], we delude and lead ourselves astray, and the Truth [which the Gospel presents] is not in us [does not dwell in our hearts]. If we [freely] admit that we have sinned and confess our sins, He is faithful and just (true to His own nature and promises) and will forgive our sins [dismiss our lawlessness] and [continuously] cleanse us from all unrighteousness [everything not in conformity to His will in purpose, thought, and action]" (1 John 1:8-9).

I explained, "As Jesus' followers, if we make mistakes, we can admit our error, accept God's forgiveness, and let Him change the behavior. We do need to cooperate with Him and follow His leading, but God is the One who carries us through the process."

As you trust God and follow His Spirit's leading, no one can condemn you. If anyone looks down on you—his or her attitude is not from God, no matter who he or she is.

Did you confess your mistakes, accept God's forgiveness, and decide to cooperate with His Spirit? If you stopped doing wrong, this is proof of restoration. As God's child, you don't have to hang your head in shame!

New Christians sometimes mature slowly and make mistakes along the way. They are still equal members of God's family. God doesn't promise us that we'll never fail. He only promises that He'll be there to pick us up. He's a Father who loves all His children and provides a level playing field. He values us equally with all believers. We're all accepted in Christ.

"There is [now no distinction] neither Jew nor Greek, there is neither slave nor free, there is not male and female; for you are all one in Christ Jesus" (Gal. 3:28).

I am not more valuable than you; you are not more valuable than me. Occupational, financial, or marital status provides no loss or gain of personal worth as a Christian. It often seems otherwise in this world, but in God's eyes we're equally important.

Christians are not exempt from betrayal, deception, or victimization, but God has the power to completely restore us. God is our loving Father, and He desires wholeness and success for His children.

Jesus promised: "I have told you these things, so that in Me you may have [perfect] peace and confidence. In the world you have tribulation and trials and distress and frustration; but be of good cheer [take courage, be confident, certain, undaunted]! For I have overcome the world. [I have deprived it of power to harm you and have conquered it for you.]" (John 16:33).

If you have accepted Christ, don't accept condemnation from anyone, even religious people. You no longer have a right to condemn yourself either. Listen to your self-talk. Are you kind to yourself? Or do you tear yourself down? You can never feel God's truth—that you have infinite value—until you stop beating yourself up.

Christ frees us from condemnation. "God made him [Jesus] who had no sin to be sin for us, so that in him we might become the righteousness of God" (2 Cor. 5:21, NIV).

"As high as the heavens are above the earth, so great is his love for those who fear him; as far as the east is from the west, so far has he removed our transgressions from us" (Ps. 103:11-12, NIV).

God's opinion is the only one that counts. Your past has no power over you.

Forget the Past

"Thus says the Lord, Who makes a way in the sea and a path through the mighty waters . . . Do not [earnestly] remember the former things; neither consider the things of old. Behold, I am doing a new thing! Now it springs forth; do you not perceive and know it and will you not give heed to it? I will even make a way in the wilderness and rivers in the desert" (Isa. 43:16, 18-19).

"I am still not all I should be but I am focusing all my energies on this one thing: Forgetting the past and looking forward to what lies ahead, I strain to reach the end of the race and receive the prize for which God is calling us up to heaven because of what Christ Jesus did for us" (Phil. 3:13-14, TLB).

Let go of your past. Whether it's positive or negative, it's over. Focusing on the past distracts us from the present, and we need all our mental and emotional energy to make the most of today.

In Christ, you're free from your past. Don't let your past define you forever.

If God leads you to share a past deliverance—wonderful. God often uses those stories. But if He doesn't lead you to share your past, don't. Either way, you'll be released to live fully in the present.

We chain ourselves to the past when we lug it around with us. Let it go! Let others know of God's amazing work in your life now. Why eat old fruit when you can eat fresh?

"My heart is not proud, O LORD, my eyes are not haughty; I do not concern myself with great matters or things too wonderful for me. But I have stilled and quieted my soul; like a weaned child with its mother, like a weaned child is my soul within me" (Ps. 131:1-2, NIV).

Children's light hearts are unencumbered by burdens and responsibilities. They know how to "cast their cares." Childlike faith keeps them free. Children with their trusting hearts believe their parents will carry them—physically, emotionally, and financially. A child will jump into a trusted parent's arms.

God wants you to trust Him enough to be open with Him. He wants you to feel safe to come to Him so He can deliver you from shame. Take a jump of faith into His open arms. He will carry you through your daily emotional struggles.

"Humble yourselves [feeling very insignificant] in the presence of the Lord, and He will exalt you [He will lift you up and make your lives significant]" (James 4:10).

Checklist to Accept God's Rescuing Presence

1. Are you willing to let Jesus into the dark areas of your emotions?
2. If not, what's stopping you?
3. What have you done to try to resolve your problem? If your strategies haven't worked, what makes you think they'll work in the future?
4. Are you willing to stop handling your problem the same way you always have?
5. Are you willing to face your struggles with God's help rather than run away?
6. Are you willing to wait on God to rescue you and not give in to your old ways of coping?
7. Has God helped you in the past? Was it because He was impressed with you or because you sincerely sought His help?
8. Are you willing to let God take over and restore you?
9. Is there something preventing you from opening your heart to God's presence? If you need help to trust Him more, ask for His help and assurance.
10. Is there anything else you can depend on as much as the One who created you?
11. What will it take for you to hand over the controls of your life?
12. Wouldn't it be easier to let God help you now?

Prayer of Acceptance

Father God, thank You for reaching out to me in love. Thank You for sending Your Son to invade the darkness and bring me into Your light.

I welcome You into the midst of my struggle with _____ [anger, fear, loneliness, rejection, resentment, or so on].

This struggle is too much for me, and I can't resolve it on my own. I submit to You, Lord. I know You'll help me. Enable me to trust You enough to keep this door open as I wait for Your deliverance. In Jesus' name. Amen.

4

Faith in Action
Wings of Hope

Albert woke up. The bedbugs had won again. Every time he turned the lights off, they attacked him in his bed, which was the couch in the living room. It was a cold morning in the Jewish neighborhood in Brooklyn, New York. The run-down apartment was never warm enough in winter.

When he was small, his older brother, Louis, died when a delivery truck hit him. Albert believed his parents lost their "golden child" and were left with him, the "ugly duckling." His parents were traumatized, depressed, and unable to reassure him. His life journey started with a lot of emotional baggage. He suffered from severe asthma and poor eyesight and was a high school dropout.

Across the street was a Christian mission to the Jews, with youth programs that included lively activities and music. His mother told him he could go and enjoy the meetings—"but don't believe anything they tell you." However, the encouraging stories and songs pierced his heart, and when Albert was 14, he gave his life to Jesus at a gospel meeting house.

He went home and told his family, "Hallelujah! Praise the Lord—I'm saved!" At first his parents thought he was making fun of the Christians, but when they realized he was serious, they almost disowned him. For three years he and his parents lived with an uneasy truce.

When he was 17 he tried to join the Army, Navy, and Marines, but none would take him because of his poor eyesight. The only job he could find was in a factory, polishing cheap chocolates so they would look more expensive.

At this point in his life Albert knew his only possibility for success would be for God to carry him through. He knew he would have to depend totally on His power.

He wanted to serve God but didn't feel adequate. One day he prayed, "God, You asked many smarter people to serve You, but some turned You down. I'm volunteering to take one of their places."

He felt God telling him, "You can't serve Me without an education."

Albert heard about a Christian high school in Toccoa Falls, Georgia, but doubted they would let him in. He decided to apply anyway and the next day sent a "seriously misspelled" letter to Toccoa Falls. He was thrilled and amazed when they accepted him—but he had no money for tuition and no support from his family.

That September he left home to go to school "by faith." Albert had only enough money to pay for his first month at school. He didn't know if he could succeed and told God, "If they reject me or throw me out, there's nothing I can do—but I promise You I won't quit! God was faithful and intervened many times, sometimes in miraculous ways.

God opened his mind to learn, and he graduated from high school, then Houghton College and seminary. In college he met and married my mom, Lee Tenison, who lovingly supports him as they travel and minister together.

Albert is my dad. He pastored large churches in the United States and Canada, published his autobiography, *A Brooklyn Jew Meets Jesus*, and currently teaches on the "Messianic Perspectives" Christian radio program. At the end of his testimony he often remarks, "Think what my life would have been if I hadn't accepted Jesus. My uncles had wanted to set me up with a newsstand in the New York subway system, where crime is frequent. Thank the Lord, that never happened. If you were to have passed me working there, you would never have imagined that such a dispirited man could have been a pastor and evangelist."[1]

How different my dad's life would have been if he hadn't walked in faith!

The fourth key to emotional freedom is to put your faith in action.

How might your circumstances change if you give God permission to unleash His power in your life? God has every resource to unburden and transform lives. This path to life and freedom is open to everyone.

King David

The gold standard for heart connection with God is King David of the Old Testament. In Psalms David pours out his emotions to the King of creation. When David was sad, he moaned and howled in despair until God answered. When afraid, he fixed his trust upon God until deliverance came. When angry, he yelled to God to hunt down his enemies and destroy them. And when he was happy, David sang to his God day and night. No wonder God called him "a man after my own heart" (Acts 13:22, NIV).

"He chose David his servant and took him from the sheep pens; from tending the sheep he brought him to be the shepherd of his people Jacob, of Israel his inheritance. And David shepherded them with integrity of heart; with skillful hands he led them" (Ps. 78:70-72, NIV).

"Integrity of heart" is another way to say "emotional honesty."

With David there was no hesitation, no self-editing, just raw, unfettered emotion, poured out in trust, until God rescued him and cleaned up the mess. David didn't give in to his emotions— he waited for God to act on his behalf. David knew God would fight his battles for him, just as a little boy would trust his dad to defend him.

In one of David's songs he writes, "Trust in, lean on, rely on, and have confidence in him at all times, you people; pour out your hearts before Him. God is a refuge for us (a fortress and a high tower). Selah [pause, and calmly think of that]!" (Ps. 62:8).

King David was not taking matters into his own hands or allowing his emotions to rage out of control. Instead, he waited on the Lord in total openness and humility. David had plenty of time on the quiet Judean hillside watching his sheep before he became king—time to commune with God and to let Him search his heart. The God of Abraham, Isaac, and Jacob became his God also, not just in word but with every beat of his shepherd's heart.

David experienced the rewards of waiting on God to deliver him. In song after song, he reported God's answers and faithfulness. David was one of the greatest kings the world ever knew. His secret was complete spiritual and emotional dependence upon God.

"I call with all my heart; answer me, O LORD, and I will obey your decrees. I call out to you; save me and I will keep your statutes. I rise before dawn and cry for help; I have put my hope in your word. My eyes stay open through the watches of the night, that I may meditate on your promises" (Ps. 119:145-148, NIV).

A Balanced Life

"But seek for (aim at and strive after) first of all His kingdom, and His righteousness (His way of doing and being right), and then all these things taken together will be given you besides" (Matt. 6:33).

Whenever we trust or seek after anyone or anything before God, our lives will be out of balance. Our Creator designed our lives to spin in perfect balance only as we rest in His love. Dependence on alcohol, drugs, or any addiction will lead to disaster. Even overanalyzing situations can lead to distress, because we trust our own logic rather than trusting God.

Tim and Suzanne, a couple I know, went through a long, dark night of the soul when their daughter, Amy, struggled with anorexia for two excruciating years. They tried many expensive treatments and prayed a lot.

Sometimes suffering makes us aware of how helpless we are. When we come to the end of our own resources, we finally allow God to be in control. By suffering we learn to walk by faith and not by sight (See 2 Cor. 5:7).

God will see us through step by step as we look to Him alone for direction.

Amy has maintained a healthy weight for more than two

years now. She recently toured with a singing group that promotes positive values, and she was asked to tell her story of recovery at each performance.

Suzanne leads a support group for parents of anorexic children. She knows she doesn't have the answers, but she knows the one who does.

That family learned to let God carry them through.

We can let God carry us every day. Then, when we need help, we'll already be in His arms. He'll strengthen us, support us, and enable us to face anything.

No Higher Position

"You are a chosen people, a royal priesthood, a holy nation, a people belonging to God, that you may declare the praises of him who called you out of darkness into his wonderful light" (1 Pet. 2:9, NIV).

When you invited Jesus into your heart, you're a royal priest also. King, queen, princess or prince—no higher position exists in the world of people. Priest, intercessor—no higher position exists in the kingdom of God. In Christ you have the highest status and position possible.

"God raised us up with Christ and seated us with him in the heavenly realms in Christ Jesus, in order that in the coming ages he might show the incomparable riches of his grace, expressed in his kindness to us in Christ Jesus. For it is by grace you have been saved, through faith—and this not from yourselves, it is the gift of God—not by works, so that none can boast" (Eph. 2:6-9, NIV).

When we invite God into every area of our hearts, we begin to see everything from His perspective.

Do you treat yourself as someone with a high position? Or do you belittle yourself? You can believe in yourself, because you believe in God and He supports you. Confidence in God's love will enable you to walk on high places.

> *Lord, lift me up and let me stand,*
> *By faith, on heaven's tableland.*
> *A higher plane than I have found—*
> *Lord, plant my feet on higher ground.*
> *—Johnson Oatman Jr.*

In Christ we're already on higher ground, but our emotions often lag behind. Our spirits are seated with Christ by the right hand of the Father, but our emotions may still be in the pits.

Breakthroughs come as we invite Jesus into each area of our hearts. When we come to Him in radical honesty and expose our hearts to the depths of His love, we'll be truly healed. The struggle is simply not a struggle anymore.

Checklist to Keep Your Heart Open to God

1. Do you believe God is your best friend?
2. Do you realize it's safe to be totally transparent with God?
3. Are you a friend to yourself?
4. Do you believe you have a high position in Christ?
5. Where do you still struggle?
6. Are you willing to invite God to daily be in charge of each area with which you struggle?
7. Do you believe God will heal you?
8. Can you identify any hurts or fears that keep your heart's door blocked?
9. Are you willing to talk with Him about any of these blocks?
10. Are you willing to come to God in honesty, admit you can't change yourself, and let Him change you?
11. Do you need to stop talking about your past and place it in God's hands?
12. Will you trust God with a seemingly hopeless area in your life?

Prayer to Open Heart Doors

Lord, I praise You that You provided a way of hope and freedom for me. I humbly come to You and admit that I need to be emotionally honest with You. Give me the courage by Your grace to see darkness within my heart and continually bring my emotions to You for cleansing and healing. Shine the light of Your truth into all the places in my heart. I invite You to enter into each painful area. Help me keep my heart's door open.

I believe Your only motivation in dealing with me is love. I will trust and follow You. Thank You for paying the price for my freedom. Lift me above the cares of this life. I pray this in the merciful name of Jesus. Amen.

PART 2

Keys to Freedom from Strongholds of Heavy Burdens

Fortress

I built myself a stronghold in the shadow of my pain,
Strengthened my resolve and did not show the strain,
In darkness tried to hide the fears crouching within,
Erected walls to keep hurt out and to keep love in.

Waiting while the years flowed by; time is never still,
In my fortress strong and high I lived with iron will.
My heart grew cold and lonely; I could not understand
How to escape the prison built with my own hand.

One day I heard Him call me just outside the gate.
He said "I've come to save you—you have no time to wait.
The winter is now past—the rain over and done.
Flowers appear upon the earth; the time to sing is come.

"Come outside your prison, and take Me by the hand.
The fortress you are living in is built upon the sand."
I ran outside to meet Him although I was afraid.
The walls crashed behind me—it almost was too late.

Now the One I love watches over me each day.
Now I never am alone—He carries me always.
When foes or fears assail I need only to pray.
I do not need a fortress—Jesus is the One who saves.

—Robin Martens

5

Confess

What Burdens Do You Carry?

Scripture does not address depression, anxiety, addictions, alcoholism, obsessions, panic, or personality disorders. But the Bible does address burdens and how to release them. Burdens are built-up, impacted, negative emotions—toxic soul sludge.

Burdens are heavy, dark, and painful emotional loads of anger, bitterness, irritation, fear, panic, anxiety, depression, and sadness. We aren't aware of all the burdens we carry because our hearts and minds can't handle too much at one time.

These feelings annoy us, and we want to rid ourselves of them as soon as possible. But if we repress our emotions instead of acknowledging them and then letting them go, we prevent our hearts from healing and accumulate heavy burdens.

During Sarah's fourth counseling session, she blurted out, "I feel like my depression is a monster I can't control sometimes. Some of the depressing feelings are gone now, and I know God is helping me. The depression isn't as extreme as it once was, but it's still there. I feel more of God's love now, but I know I'm not quite where I need to be."

I told her, "When we deny our emotions over a long period of time, they can gain monstrous proportions in our minds and become a stronghold of heavy burdens. These strongholds become cemented in place by addictions, distractions, and defenses—whatever we do to avoid those emotions. If your depression is the result of heart wounds that need healing, then you must release the burdens of hurt to begin healing."

I asked Sarah, "If you had a knife that could cut your depression off, would you use it?"

"Definitely," she exclaimed.

"Do you know God loves the part of you that struggles with depression?"

"How could He? It's such a mess."

"God loves you, and that goes for every part of you. Jesus paid the price to heal your spirit, soul, and emotions. If you can get the part of you that feels like a monster to come to Jesus for help, it will stop feeling that way. Jesus can clean the poison out of that part of your heart and mind and heal you."

Over the years, I've talked to many clients who had a hard time praying when they were depressed, anxious, angry, or acting out their addiction. An alcoholic doesn't feel spiritual when he or she is headed for the bar. A woman struggling with pornography or lust has a hard time talking to God because of shame. In the midst of rage, prayer is the last thing on our minds. However, times like these can be the most effective times to pray.

Sarah's emotional framework was split—she vacillated between two points of view. One day life seemed great; the next day life seemed hopeless. The face she presented to others was calm and seemed happy, and when she was in this frame of mind she knew God loved her. The other burdened heart condition she fell into was depressed, angry, and fearful. With this clouded view she saw God and others as distant and uncaring. When she was depressed, she felt hatred toward herself and rejected herself.

Persistent, conflicting emotional states must be brought into the light to heal. Is the view the same from your mind and from your emotions? If not, you may have spots in your heart that have not been touched by God's light, warmth, and healing. Each emotional door must be opened by an act of will. The door opens when we admit we need rescue, believe that God can and will take our burdens away, and ask Him to do so.

When we bring the darkest part of our hearts to Jesus, we're on the brink of freedom. Let the part of you that panics, despairs, rages, obsesses, hates, swears, lusts, or wants to give in to addiction form a relationship with God by becoming honest, developing trust, and accepting His help. As He begins to clean out the hurt, anger, and sin, you'll begin to function the way God originally intended. He wants to transform you.

Some don't want to engage in the struggle to bring these

thoughts and feelings directly to God. True, it may be a painful or long process, but if you don't invite God to intervene, you could fight the same problems the rest of your life. And sometimes God removes our burdens quickly and one begins to sense the freedom He gives right away.

You may experience strong emotions such as grief, fear, or anger as you let go of your burdens, but keep your emotions open to God. In Joel 2:13 this process is described: "Rend your hearts . . . and return to the Lord, your God, for He is gracious and merciful, slow to anger, and abounding in loving-kindness."

If you feel overwhelmed by the process, seek the care of a professional Christian counselor or doctor.

It's important to be responsible, to fulfill work obligations, and take care of your home and family. Doing what's right no matter how you feel is the foundation to true emotional freedom.

"God is not a God of disorder but of peace . . . everything should be done in a fitting and orderly way" (1 Cor. 14:33, 40).

God Wants to Carry Your Burdens

What's weighing you down? Do you feel anxious, irritable, or sad? God wants you to shift that weight to Him.

Some burdens are like pebbles—very small when carried one at a time, but if they accumulate, your load becomes heavy. Other burdens are so heavy right from the start that you may feel as if you're pinned beneath a boulder.

What are the frustrating, burdensome areas of your life? You can have a new start. It's best to start with the areas that bother you the most today. Look at the parts of your life where nothing's growing or where you have the most emotional pain. This is the top layer that God can deal with first and is the easiest to get at.

This layer can be addictions that cover emotions you're not completely aware of. People who are happy don't usually get entangled in severe addictions. Every addiction or compulsion in your life is covering a small or large area of pain.

The more emotional pain we want to numb out or distract ourselves from, the more extreme the addiction or compulsion becomes. We don't realize we're still damaged; the wound is still there causing problems even if it's numbed out. It's like taking morphine so we don't feel the pain of a broken wrist instead of having it set properly. That wrist will continue to cause tremendous problems until it's properly healed.

Emotional honesty with God is crucial. Intellectual honesty alone will not permit Him to work fully in your life. Your emotions, especially the most painful ones, give you valuable information about where you are now. They tell you if you're still damaged from past hurts and when you start to be injured now. Your hand jerks back if it gets too close to a fire—the pain warns that you're too close. Your physical nerves don't bother you when you're healthy and not in danger. Your emotions work in a similar way.

Obvious burdens are constantly on our minds: worries about a rebellious teen, a serious illness, or the loss of a loved one. But many burdens are not obvious yet still affect us profoundly. Underlying anger or irritation can boil over at a moment's notice and scald those who are close to us. Buried guilt robs us of our joy, and hurts from the past surface when we least expect it.

Whether we call them burdens, blind spots, mental blocks, or sore spots, they're all similar. These are all emotional reactions to frustration, loss, or trauma that we've not let go. We can recognize burdens by noticing patterns of emotions or behavior. When we notice a pattern of overreacting with anxiety, depression, or rage, then we know we have some old emotions controlling us. Intense reactions signify burdens—unhealed emotional wounds.

If you enjoy writing, journaling can be beneficial in your walk toward freedom. In my journal I write down prayers, thanksgiving for answers, and daily events.

However, if you want to confess and release emotional poison as you journal, use a three-ring binder or an inexpensive spiral notebook. After you write about your anger, hurt, rejection, lust, or whatever you feel, ask God to forgive you and to help you forgive others, and then throw the paper away.

The tool of writing out underlying emotions is a powerful way to break out of strongholds. As you bring your burdens out of the darkness into the light and on to the paper, the way to freedom becomes more obvious.

When a new situation causes you emotional turmoil, it can be helpful to journal your feelings or write a letter to whoever upset you. After you vent and forgive, make sure you throw the paper away. It considerably speeds up the process of releasing present burdens.

If you don't enjoy writing, you can still vent your emotions in prayer, confessing and releasing them.

Most obstacles in our lives are emotional in nature. Ignored emotional hurts can grow into mountains, but God's power can bring them crashing down. We can explore our emotional dimension with God's help. He's big enough to handle anything contained within our hearts and souls. God has carried many people through problems like the ones you're facing. He'll carry you to freedom.

Seeing Burdens

Take the light of God's Word and shine it on your emotional reality. The psalmist wrote, "Your word is a lamp to my feet and a light to my path" (Ps. 119:105).

If we were to wander outside in the dark, we might run into a wall or walk off a cliff. Our emotional dimension is like an invisible landscape, filled with boulders, mountains, and narrow passageways. We're in serious trouble if we can't see where we're going.

When I've counseled homeless women, I've been amazed that they often deny any serious problems and think changing their circumstances would solve everything. Sometimes when these women were close to being approved for welfare or were ready to move into an apartment, they disappeared. I heard they moved to a far-away place where they hoped life would be better. But they often landed in another shelter or destructive relationship and returned in a few months without having made any real progress. They were stuck in the strongholds of their hearts and kept repeating self-destructive behavior patterns. When we move or start new relationships, we tend to carry our burdens with us.

If we look honestly at our burdens so that we can get a handle on them and give them to God for healing and cleansing, we make a huge step toward freedom. Our hearts must be open in order to see our true condition and the spiritual and emotional doors to freedom.

"You say, I am rich; I have prospered and grown wealthy, and I am in need of nothing; and you do not realize and understand that you are wretched, pitiable, poor, blind and naked. Therefore I counsel you to purchase from Me gold refined and tested by fire, that you may be [truly] wealthy, and white clothes to clothe you and to keep the shame of your nudity from being seen, and salve to put on your eyes, that you may see" (Rev. 3:17-18).

In the preceding verses Jesus is speaking to Christians. If we aren't aware of the pain we carry, we also won't notice how our burdens stunt emotional growth, cause blind spots, and poison relationships.

If we could see how people feel emotionally, we would understand them better. We have compassion for obvious physical wounds but not invisible emotional or spiritual wounds. We tend to lose patience with someone who always seems down. We're disgusted when someone who seems rational loses emotional control.

But God understands completely.

What if we woke up tomorrow and saw others the way God sees them? Beneath the polished exteriors we would see broken hearts that are overwhelmed with burdens. Then we would understand why some people are overly sensitive or why it's hard for them to cope with day-to-day living.

If your arm was out of joint and extremely painful, you wouldn't tolerate even the slightest bump or pressure. Similarly, some people react intensely if they feel "bumped" emotionally.

There's no excuse for us if we harm others by our reactions. We're responsible for our behavior no matter how damaged we are. However, understanding hidden hurts does explain some things. An emotionally healthy person withstands the stresses of life more easily than someone with a smashed heart.

Some carry burdens so gigantic that it's amazing they function at all. Living with a burdened heart is like trying to dance with leaden feet.

God built us to carry a load that He's lightened for us. We have a limited capacity to store buried emotions. When we're young, there's usually plenty of room in our emotional storage tank. But when this capacity overflows because of trauma, loss, or ongoing difficulties, it becomes difficult or impossible to control the power of the emotions. Depression, panic-attacks, rage, severe addictions, or obsessions are all signs of stored, dissociated emotions overflowing in a person's life.

When denied emotions build up, they can become so powerful that they seem out of control. Sadness, anger, or anxiety can snowball into depression, rage, or panic attacks. During a mid-life crisis, overflowing, pent-up emotions can destroy a family, but after the emotional storm passes, the person often wonders why he or she reacted.

Overwhelming emotions are usually what push someone to seek counseling—when their usual coping skills just won't work for them anymore. Their emotions won't heal until the feelings are owned, processed, and released.

The healing of emotions is similar to draining the poison from a wound. Sometimes the process is short, and sometimes it takes longer, but the relief and freedom afterward are worth letting God carry you through.

"I know that nothing good dwells within me, that is, in my flesh. I can will what is right, but I cannot perform it. [I have the intention and urge to do what is right, but no power to carry it out.]" (Rom. 7:18).

As we read the Word of God and are exposed to His truth, our human inadequacies become woefully evident. The truth that sets us free is not only the truth in the Scripture but also our having the courage to see the truth within our own hearts. Only then will we successfully apply God's truth to our own reality and become genuinely free.

God already knows what's in our hearts, but He's waiting for us to be willing to face it. When we're hurt, afraid, or angry, we can confess it and give it to God right away. Sin comes in when we try to use our own devices to handle our hurts. It's the sin of not trusting in God to heal and free us, the sin of pride and self-sufficiency. Being hurt by someone else is not a sin. It becomes our sin when we determine to handle the hurt on our own without God's help.

God doesn't want us to suffer and carry heavy burdens. He has the power to cleanse us and remove our burdens. When we become aware of an unpleasant or sinful emotion or thought process that keeps recurring in our lives, we should rejoice. God is shining light on it so we can get free.

How Burdens Develop

Instead of bringing anxiety, panic, anger, sadness, or rage to God as King David did in the Psalms, we often push those emotions out of our conscious mind. When we don't want to admit we have negative emotions or attitudes, we continue to carry them. We dissociate, which basically means we pretend the feelings aren't there. We lie to ourselves when we choose to be unaware of our negative feelings.

When we experience small hurts, we usually can release them without too much trouble. God built a processing system within us to let go of negative emotions. If a friend is grumpy with us, a few days later we might hardly remember the incident. However, our hearts become overloaded when we're traumatized or if everyday hurts are not resolved.

An accident victim in shock feels no pain. Something similar occurs when we're in severe emotional pain. Our brains go into shock because of overwhelming emotional pain. Instead of processing the pain and letting it go, our brains set it aside to be dealt with at a safer time. If we don't face and process trauma, the pain stays inside, festers, grows, and can poison our attitudes and relationships.

Emotions are real. They are chemical responses our body produces as our minds react to the world around us. Emotions can be stored as burdens, or they can be released. Only when we release the emotions are we able to truly heal.

Ask God to reveal the burdens you carry. Trauma or shame can be hard to face, but we must admit and face our burdens before we can let them go. God may reveal a lie we believed, a hurt that still hasn't healed, or emotional thought patterns we're ashamed to see. It isn't pleasant to have the darkness we've been living in revealed to us.

Many persons never get free because they refuse to experience the pain of seeing what lies within their hearts. Confessing exactly what's in our hearts and experiencing the emotion is the only way out. However, it's sometimes possible to get through the process quickly with God's help.

We need to realize that the pain we carry is not who we are. Burdens don't need to be a permanent part of our personalities; we weren't born with them. The emotional pain we carry came from outside us from others hurting and disappointing us.

Burdens are just stored emotional reactions. They're like mud on a car—they can be washed off. Many continue to carry heavy burdens throughout life, but it's unnecessary. If old memories aren't healed, they may continue to cause excruciating pain when we're reminded of them. Some people accumulate burdens and become increasingly bitter, sad, or fearful as each year passes. But some learn to release burdens and radiate peace and joy.

Remember that we're saved by the grace of Jesus, not by anything good we do. The shameful, obsessive, or confused parts of our lives can't be too bad for God to save. Jesus loved us and died for us when we were yet sinners, and that includes every part of our broken hearts. Our emotional patterns can't be too sinful for God to tenderly forgive us and set us free.

"God shows and clearly proves His [own] love for us by the fact that while we were still sinners Christ (the Messiah, the Anointed One) died for us. Therefore, since we are now justified (acquitted, made righteous, and brought into right relationship with God) by Christ's blood, how much more [certain is it that] we shall be saved by Him from the indignation and wrath of God. For if while we were enemies we were reconciled to God through the death of His Son, it is much more [certain], now that we are reconciled, that we shall be saved (daily delivered from sin's dominion) through His [resurrection] life" (Rom. 5:8-10).

If God loved us when we were still sinners, how much more does He love us now that we're His children? How much more does He want to free us from our chains? Jesus died to free us! All He asks is that we be honest with Him and open the doors of our hearts to Him—not just once but every day, not just with large problems but with tiny problems as well. Nothing is too small for the One who created the atom. Nothing is too large for the One who created the universe.

Emergency Exits

One of Sarah's emergency exits was obsessing about her weight and diet, which helped her avoid underlying feelings for a while.

I encouraged her to postpone binge eating and worrying and instead face her feelings—journaling the emotions that surfaced. By venting safely, she was able to reduce the force of emotion behind her weight problem and obsession. Sarah told me she felt miserable when she put off eating or worrying about dieting, but if she had a good cry, she felt relief.

Our coping behaviors weave thread by thread into our lives until they become almost unbreakable. Some are healthful routines, such as exercising or working. But some are destructive practices that can become strongholds. These strongholds are habits, addictions, and obsessions. At first they seem to help us handle our burdens, but if they become extreme, they imprison and can destroy us.

Overeating, overspending, overdoing, overmedicating, or over-anything can become our emergency exit—or addiction of choice. When we continually avoid painful emotions, we only increase our pain.

When you're angry, sad, scared, or even lustful or hateful, you have an opportunity to allow God to invade and change your heart. The burdened part of your heart—with all its pain, irrationality, or extreme thinking—needs to speak directly to God. Remember—He loves you even when you're hurting, angry, anxious, or out of control with addiction.

Where do you run when you hurt? Who or what *must* you have in your life? Whatever you depend on to relieve and distract you from emotional pain or discontent may be keeping you from finding freedom.

Most people in today's society dread pain and avoid it at all costs. We medicate our aches and pains with all kinds of drugs. Some medications are wonderful. Thank God that antibiotics, polio vaccines, and antidepressants are available if needed. However, it isn't always best to avoid pain. Pain gives us valuable messages. If we anesthetize all pain, we may ultimately be damaged because we aren't listening to its helpful warnings.

We were created to be dependent on God. The only healthful dependency is dependency on God. Strongholds, addictions, obsessions, and compulsions are actually all defense mechanisms with different manifestations. Alcoholism, workaholism, drug addiction, compulsive hand-washing, obsessive thoughts, or staying too busy to think—all serve the same purpose. These are distractions we use to avoid or numb our underlying emotional pain. These strongholds separate us from our own hearts and from the love and help of God.

God is our Creator; He knows what we need. If you aren't sure whether or not you trust God in a certain area, ask yourself if God is the first One you talk to when you're hurting. If you have a habit of going to someone else or something else before you go to God, then that's who or what you've placed your trust in. You won't be free until you let go of that dependency.

If you're running to someone or something besides God, you're running to someone or something with no power. Whatever you think you can't live without contributes to your misery or failure. When you depend on a crutch instead of God, your supports will splinter under you.

When we pull away from God, it's by our own choice. We lock Him out and then wonder where He is. God respects our free will and does not force open the doors of our hearts. He waits to be invited in. Start depending on Him in the hard areas of your life. Open the door, avoid your other dependencies, and wait on the Lord. He'll save you.

Take Inventory

When I meet with a client for the first time, I listen for the ways the person comforts or distracts himself or herself. The number and intensity of his or her distractions, addictions, or obsessions indicates how heavy the person's burdens are. Heavy burdens require more intense distractions to numb the pain.

Addictions are created when we consistently use a substance, person, or activity to avoid our feelings. When we continually avoid negative emotions, they become stored in different rooms in our hearts and minds. These become blind spots or burden strongholds. When we use our own mental devices to keep emotions in darkness, we're not under God's control in that area. We're not allowing God's love, grace, and mercy to cleanse and heal us.

Some distractions are beneficial when kept in balance. It's good to forget your troubles for a while and immerse yourself in a wholesome book or movie. But extreme distractions are a dense fog covering the truth. The fog needs to be lifted in order to see where we can move forward. When we reduce or stop our distractions, the painful force behind our burdens will surface so we can bring it to God for release and healing.

Usually it's hard to completely stop addictions or obsessions. Try to reduce the distracting behavior by putting it off for a while, and then observe and journal your emotions. The root cause of your addiction will be revealed. It takes courage to face and release underlying pain. Pray for strength to go through the pain and get free.

The following is a partial list of dependencies, addictions, and obsessions we may keep ourselves bound with. Do you use one or more of these strategies to distract yourself from distress? Pay attention to how extreme your addictions or obsessions are. This indicates how much energy it takes to numb the pain you carry.

Checklist to Identify Burden Strongholds

- Depending too much on people—always calling friends to complain rather than using that energy to seek God, to face and resolve the problem
- Obsessions with food—undereating or overeating
- Obsessing about money—worrying about bills or dreaming about winning a sweepstakes to the point it distracts you from what you need to do
- Caffeine addiction—overdependence on caffeine to get you through the day
- Sugar addiction—a never-ending cycle of craving and eating sugary foods
- Drug addiction
- Alcohol addiction
- Focusing on other people's problems instead of facing your own

- Shopping addiction—spending more than you can afford
- Gambling addiction
- Sexual addiction
- Intellectualizing about problems rather than feeling and facing emotions
- Creating chaos
- Reading addiction
- Smoking addiction
- Television addiction
- Newspaper and news addiction
- Work addiction
- Entertainment addiction
- Worry addiction

Prayer to Confess Burden Strongholds

Father, I praise You for Your power—power great enough to create the universe. My struggles are nothing for You to handle. I bring them to You in trust. Forgive me for trying to handle my burdens [or addictions] *alone. Forgive me for looking to lifeless substances or limited human beings to help me. Forgive me for not letting You help me in this area.*

I know You desire and are able to deliver me. Shine Your light into my heart and show me what's there. I open my heart to You and confess the exact nature of my struggle from this hurting place within my heart. [Journal exactly what your extreme emotions or addictions would say if they could talk—use paper you can throw away.] *Help me understand that You're my friend, even when I believe my emotions or actions are monstrous. I pray and believe You'll forgive me for wrong attitudes and behaviors. Thank You for Your forgiveness. I believe You'll deliver me from burdens and release me from this stronghold. In Jesus' name I pray. Amen.*

6

Believe

God's Love Will Release You

———

"**Lean on, trust in, and be confident** in the Lord with all your heart and mind and do not rely on your own insight or understanding. In all your ways know, recognize, and acknowledge Him, and He will direct and make straight and plain your paths" (Prov. 3:5-6).

Sarah settled into her regular spot on the couch. She seemed stronger and more hopeful. Outside, cold November winds scattered a light snow. The sun shone intensely, glinting off the cars in the parking lot, but failed to warm the air.

She said, "This week I realized I never really trusted the Lord in the areas I've been extremely ashamed of. I was hurt when I was young and never opened up my depression and anxiety to God. I was angry that He didn't help me before. I prayed for Him to remove the problem but never felt able to completely trust Him. I'm ready to work on this."

I was happy to hear her say this, because I knew we couldn't progress unless Sarah decided to trust God with her underlying pain.

We can't rest in God's care if we don't trust Him. We won't stay close to someone we don't trust. God can't help us if we don't let Him, because He respects our free will. At times we may prevent Him from helping us because we have trouble trusting Him. God said, "My people are destroyed for lack of knowledge" (Hos. 4:6).

Confessing the truth in our hearts and changing direction can be scary. It's as if we've been on a train all our lives, chugging around the same old track. Although we don't like the track we're on, it's familiar and comfortable. When we see and confess our sins and change direction, suddenly our train is on a new track. We fear the unknown, not knowing for sure if we're heading for a better place or if the tracks will dead-end and the train will fall off a cliff somewhere! We have to trust where God is leading us.

Faith in God is the victory that overcomes the world. Faith is a powerful key to freedom. "Now faith is the assurance (the confirmation, the title deed) of the things [we] hope for, being the proof of things [we] do not see and the conviction of their reality [faith perceiving as real fact what is not revealed to the senses]" (Heb. 11:1).

Faith is like a door we can open or shut. When we trust enough to open the door of faith, we're allowing God's power and goodness to flow into our lives.

Fear is like a door also. Fear is actually a type of faith—that bad things will happen. Not trusting God can open a door of fear in our lives, allowing the negative to flow in.

We can't control everything—only God is in full control. But we have more ability than we realize to allow God or Satan to work in our lives by the doors we open and close by our free will.

We're not gods, and we can't control our destiny. However, when we open the door of faith, we invite God to do good things in our lives. When we open the door of fear, we're more vulnerable to bad things happening. Yes, God can and often will protect us anyway. However, it's important to realize this principle. It can make a great difference in our lives.

They Just Want to Keep Their Problems, Right?

Larry, one of our neighbors, said to me one shining fall afternoon as we raked up red and gold leaves, "Don't you think some people like their problems? I don't think they want to let go of them. They stay stuck in emotional problems because they like attention."

I disagree with Larry. I never met anyone who doesn't want to be free. No one really enjoys suffering.

People expend a lot of time, energy, and money seeking to escape or rid themselves of distressing emotional burdens. When we meet someone who talks incessantly about his or her problems, we must realize that he or she is hoping we have an answer.

This person wants to find someone or something to bring him or her relief.

The poison of emotional hurt must be drained from our minds and hearts just as infection must be drained from a wound. Would it make sense to tell someone just to forget a deep cut showing signs of infection? That's what we do when we tell people to forget their emotional wounds. The pain is a constant or periodic reminder. We forget hurtful memories when they heal—and not before.

It's sad when Christians suffer day after day with the debilitating weight of their burdens. I'm sure it grieves God for His children to struggle on without relief when His answers are available.

People who have not faced severe difficulties may find it hard to understand those who have. And then there are those who do give their burdens to God, and they can't understand why others don't do the same.

The reason is that many truly don't know how to give their burdens to the Lord. Maybe they don't trust enough yet, or maybe they feel they've tried and it hasn't worked for them. It's not our place to judge them. Only God knows their hearts.

Many Christians may fall under the weight of their burdens and behave in ways they never thought they were capable of because they didn't know how to find their freedom.

Jesus paid for their freedom with His blood. Trusting God with our darkest feelings and thoughts is crucial in order to gain freedom.

God did not create us to live burdened, frustrated lives. His will is for us to overcome by faith. So how do we let God help us? First, we need to see more clearly what happened in our own personal history. When did we decide we could not trust?

The doors to some hearts may have closed during childhood. Even if we have great faith in some areas of our lives, we still need to trust God in other difficult areas in order to break free. Are you trusting God in the midst of every struggle? He waits until you trust enough to open the door. Then He'll walk in with His love. Light will flood in, and your world will start to change.

When Jesus healed the two blind men in Matt. 9:29-30, "He touched their eyes, saying, According to your faith and trust and reliance [on the power invested in Me] be it done to you. And their eyes were opened."

Whenever we feel lost and alone, it's usually because we aren't trusting God. The solution is to admit this and let Him forgive and cleanse us from unbelief and emotional pain.

It's necessary to grieve losses and disappointments in order to go through the door to freedom. If you try to get free without feeling any pain, it's like trying to go through a door without taking your elbow—it won't work.

The pain trapped within our hearts and minds must be felt and released in order to heal. If we understand that going through a door of pain is the way to gain freedom, we'll be more patient with the process.

God is described as a gardener who cuts away dead and diseased areas of a plant to foster healthy growth. God could also be thought of as a surgeon who removes the cancer of festering, stored emotions that are often full of sinful thoughts and attitudes. But we must trust Him and let Him work. When we jump off the operating table and say we can handle life on our own, surgery is postponed, and we continue to be burdened with cancerous emotions.

"There is no fear in love [dread does not exist], but full-grown (complete, perfect) love turns fear out of doors and expels every trace of terror! For fear brings with it the thought of punishment, and [so] he who is afraid has not reached the full maturity of love [is not yet grown into love's complete perfection]. We love Him, because He first loved us" (1 John 4:18-19).

There's a remedy for all broken, burdened hearts: God wants to take the broken pieces of our hearts, clean the burdens off, and put the pieces back together!

"He heals the brokenhearted and binds up their wounds [curing their pains and their sorrows]" (Ps. 147:3).

How Trust Develops

"When I was a child, I talked like a child, I thought like a child, I reasoned like a child; now that I have become a man, I am done with childish ways and have put them aside" (1 Cor. 13:11).

Our relationships affect our trust level as children and shape our self-concept. Usually parents love their children immensely. But they and other caring adults often fail us because of human limitations. All parents are limited in their ability to love. We're flawed beings—every family has some dysfunction. When others fail us, our ability to trust and our self-concept are damaged.

When we're young and undiscerning, we tend to absorb others' words and actions as truth about ourselves. Did your parents smile when you walked in? Did they frown? Did they ignore you? Did they have time for you? Did they treat you with respect? Were they kind and affectionate? What was their tone of voice when they spoke to you? Did they look you in the eyes? Did they hug you and tell you they loved you?

When you were a child, your family members' behavior, words, and voice tone told you many things. If they didn't act loving, attentive, or respectful to you at times, you may believe you're unworthy. You may decide you can't trust anyone to come through for you in those ways—including God.

We usually believe God is like our father or father figure. But God is totally different than any earthly father—He's loving, patient, merciful, and holy. We can open our hearts fully to God.

God can't help us with damaged, shut-down areas of our hearts unless we trust Him. Emotional abscesses need to be opened up in total honesty for God to cleanse and heal them.

When we were young, unless we had a guide, we didn't know how to reach out to God. So we chose our own way to handle overwhelming emotions. One person may withdraw from people, another may retreat into fantasy or drugs, and another may lash out in self-protective anger. Whatever habits we develop to protect ourselves can in time become our personal prison.

If your ways of coping aren't working for you, stop repeating the behavior, and allow God to intervene now. When we turn to God with an old wound, we may need to talk to Him about the deep hurt or anger we felt because we thought He abandoned us. He understands. When we seek Him, He always responds in love.

Sarah asked me a common question: "Why should I trust God now—where was He all those times I was hurt?"

"God was there, suffering with you. I don't understand why God lets us get damaged, but I know He cares for you and will bring good out of even the worst situations when you put them into His hands."

Only an enemy would rub our faces in the dirt, stomp on us, and attempt to destroy us. One of Satan's favorite tactics is to try to annihilate Christians and then convince them that God allowed it for their good. This sometimes prevents Christians from resisting Satan, because they're afraid they may be fighting God's will.

We must stand against evil. "Submit yourselves, then, to God. Resist the devil, and he will flee from you" (James 4:7, NIV).

When the focus is on God and His goodness, we'll experience true joy. If we're to trust God to be our Guide, then we have to step out in faith and start believing in who He says we are. When we meditate on the truth of God's Word, our minds and hearts are renewed.

Emotionally free people are God-conscious, not self-conscious; God-confident, not self-confident. People healed by God's grace can forget themselves and care for others.

It's hard to forget ourselves if we hate ourselves. People with the most out-of-control emotions are actually the ones who hate their anger, depression, or anxiety the most. Self-hatred creates a vicious cycle. God doesn't want us to hate or condemn anyone, even ourselves. He corrects but never condemns His children. Self-hatred chains us, but accepting God's love, forgiveness, and grace sets us free.

Sarah beat up on herself emotionally when she went off her diet. The self-hatred only caused her to despair and eat even more as "punishment" for her excess. As she invited Jesus into her struggle and accepted His forgiveness, she gradually forgave herself and escaped this destructive cycle.

When you come to God in honesty, He'll release you from burdens of self-hatred, guilt, depression, anger, and anxiety. "He is able to save to the uttermost (completely, perfectly, finally, and for all time and eternity) those who come to God through Him, since He is always living to make petition to God and intercede with Him and intervene for them" (Heb. 7:25).

Every morning we can ask for God's presence and direction in every difficult or enjoyable situation. When I admit my dependence on God, it's amazing how much smoother the day goes. Difficult work situations and even fun weekends work out better.

Anyone who sacrificed so much for your welfare doesn't want you carrying heavy burdens. His shoulders are broad enough to carry you, and He longs for you to come to Him.

Checklist for Deeper Trust

1. In what area do you have trouble trusting God?
2. When did you decide you couldn't trust God?
3. Would it be possible to decide to trust Him now? If not, why not? Are you willing to talk it over with God and see if He can help you trust again?
4. Are you willing to forgive those who damaged your ability to trust? Are you willing to stop blaming them?
5. Are you willing to take responsibility for your current attitudes, emotions, or addictions?
6. Has God helped you or someone you know with a similar problem? What makes you think He can't help you now?
7. Are you willing to confess your inability to trust and let God cleanse you from unbelief?
8. Do you pray when you struggle with an emotion or addiction, or do you try to handle it on your own?
9. Do you think you can handle your problems better than God can?
10. Do you think God doesn't want to be bothered with your problems?
11. Do you believe God loves you?
12. When you love someone, do you want to help him or her, or do you want to let him or her suffer?

Prayer of Trust

Father God, forgive me for not realizing how much You love me. Teach me to trust You. Although I've struggled for such a long time, I believe You'll do a new thing. Shine Your light upon my darkness. Reveal to me how much You love me. Open the eyes of my heart to see

Your powerful reality and Your ability to deliver me.

I don't want to walk alone anymore. Forgive me for trying to protect and medicate myself with my dependencies instead of trusting You. I thank You for Your forgiveness. Let me feel Your loving arms around me every time I feel tempted or afraid. I pray and believe You'll be with me in every duty or recreation today. I trust You to provide everything I need. I pray this in Jesus' name. Amen.

7

Accept
God's Offer

===========

"**Cast your burden on the Lord** [releasing the weight of it] and He will sustain you" (Ps. 55:22).

Sarah was miserable. "Today I hate myself, I hate my marriage, and I even feel as if I can't stand being around my daughter. What's wrong with me?"

"Sarah, we all have the same thing wrong with us. We are born imperfect into a damaging world. Jesus is the only one who can make us whole."

I helped Sarah lay these burdens of shameful thoughts and feelings at the foot of the Cross. Jesus paid the price for all her anger. As she vented, we brought each distress to God in prayer and asked Him to clean out her poisonous feelings. We asked Him to enter into each damaged place in her heart and deliver her.

Sarah prayed that God would enable her to forgive herself, her husband, and her daughter. She confessed her limited patience and ability to love, and she asked God to remove her hardheartedness and infuse His love into her heart.

"As you have therefore received Christ Jesus the Lord, so walk in Him, rooted and built up in Him and established in the faith. . . . For in Him dwells all the fullness of the Godhead bodily; and you are complete in Him, who is the head of all principality and power" (Col. 2:6-7, 9-10, NKJV).

We walk with Christ the same way we accept Him—admitting that we're nothing without Him, trusting Him to remove our burdens, and accepting His grace on a continual basis.

How did we accept Christ? Did He rescue us because of our goodness, or did He rescue us because we accepted His love and forgiveness? If we're saved by grace, why, then, do we try to heal our emotions ourselves? Why don't we come to God, admit who we truly are, and accept His grace and provision for our emotional healing?

"Come to me, all you who are weary and burdened, and I will give you rest. Take my yoke upon you and learn from me, for I am gentle and humble in heart, and you will find rest for your souls. For my yoke is easy and my burden is light" (Matt. 11:28-30, NIV).

Eve's Terrible Day

This is the day all our troubles started:

Eve wasn't happy—in spite of the sun's warmth, silky breeze, and magnificence encompassing her. A birch forest gleamed like white fire; orchids, columbine, and myrtle carpeted the glade. Golden sand embraced a crystal river flowing by with schools of glistening, silver fish. She tested the water, and wet coolness rippled over her bare feet. She sat by the river's edge, as if exhausted, and sighed.

Adam was exploring again. Something felt wrong, but what? Eve knew God created her, but she didn't like feeling so dependent. She sifted sand through her fingers. *Why can't I think for myself?* she wondered. *Who says I have to always listen to Him? I want to know what God knows.*

As always, the tree of the knowledge of good and evil beckoned to her. It sat in the garden's center, glittering like a crown jewel. The exquisite fruit drew her like a magnet.

Eve loved fruit, and her garden was full of delights. She sampled most of the fruits many times, and she was bored. It was time for a change.

She stood and shook off the sand. Her feet took her up the worn path to the heart of the garden. A serpent slithered around the trunk.

"Did God really say, 'You must not eat from any tree in the garden'?"

Eve glanced down at the snake with the flashing green diamonds cascading down his back. Snakes always talked a lot.

She responded, "We may eat fruit from the trees in the garden, but God did say, 'You must not eat fruit from the tree that is in the middle of the garden, and you must not touch it, or you will surely die.'"

"You will not surely die . . . for God knows that when you eat of it your eyes will be opened, and you will be like God, knowing good and evil" (Gen. 3:1-5, NIV). The snake gazed at her with a knowing look.

Eve pondered for a moment. *The serpent never lied to me before. Nothing ever hurts me here. Surely God won't punish me for such a small thing. I only want one little bite, and then I'll never touch it again. I just want to know what it tastes like.*

Eve stretched out her hand and grasped the smooth redness. It smelled so good! *How could anything so desirable be bad?*

Crunch! *Yum.* Eve didn't see the black thunderclouds rolling in behind her.

With that bite evil flooded into the garden. The damage would not be undone for thousands of years. Of course, if we lived in Eden, we would have done the same. Eve is the mother of our nature. We all desire independence.

We lost our trusting friendship with our Creator—we're on our own, and we're in trouble. The only way to reverse the damage is to become dependent once again.

We were not created to handle emotions in our own strength without the empowering, infilling presence of God directly impacting and healing our distress. Adam and Eve were not created to withstand sin's onslaught. Only the redeeming love of God and the power of the Cross can preserve our hearts in health and wholeness in spite of the crushing evil around us.

Our troubles stem from our thinking we can figure it all out instead of bringing everything to God in trust and humility. Only God knows what's truly right or wrong for us.

To some who were confident of their own righteousness and looked down on everybody else, Jesus told this parable: "Two men went up to the temple to pray, one a Pharisee and the other a tax collector. The Pharisee stood up and prayed about himself: 'God, I thank you that I am not like other men—robbers, evildoers, adulterers—or even like this tax collector. I fast twice a week and give a tenth of all I get.'

"But the tax collector stood at a distance. He would not even look up to heaven, but beat his breast and said, 'God, have mercy on me, a sinner.'

"I tell you that this man, rather than the other, went home justified before God. For everyone who exalts himself will be humbled, and he who humbles himself will be exalted (Luke 18:9-14, NIV).

To be justified means "to demonstrate or prove to be just, right, or valid . . . to declare free of blame; absolve . . . to free (man) of the guilt and penalty attached to grievous sin. Said only of God."[1]

We need to stop feeling good about our efforts to clean up our act, and instead allow God to justify us. "All these things My hand has made, and so all these things have come into being [by and for Me], says the Lord. But this is the man to whom I will look and have regard: he who is humble and of a broken or wounded spirit, and who trembles at My word and reveres My commands" (Isa. 66:2).

When we become humbly transparent, we can release burdens and accept God's healing. This is most possible in the midst of temptation, addiction, or obsession. You may, however, be thinking that God won't be happy with you if you talk to Him when you have a bad attitude.

Remember, though, that in 1 John 1:9 He tells us to confess our sins. In our personal war zones we can confess exactly what's within our hearts. Alcoholics don't want to pray on the way to the bar, the ill-tempered don't want to talk to God while in a rage, and it's difficult to pray when gripped by panic. But these are the most powerful times to pray. These are the times when we can fully open the doors to our hearts and accept His forgiveness and rescue. The healing is done by the grace of God through the atoning work of Jesus—not through our efforts.

When veterans suffer from panic attacks, nightmares, and flashbacks, they often find healing by remembering the war zone and reliving and then releasing those pent-up emotions.

If we wait to pray until we get our bad attitudes cleaned up, we're missing God's work in our lives. God will not force the door open.

God's Holy Spirit guides us. He will bring people to help us along for a while, but we must first depend on Him. We become spiritually and emotionally mature as we lean more on God and less on others.

Contrary to a common human belief that men and women guide their own fates, the Bible says we are but sheep in need of a shepherd (Ps. 100). However, "I have strength for all things in Christ Who empowers me [I am ready for anything and equal to anything through Him who infuses inner strength into me; I am self-sufficient in Christ's sufficiency]" (Phil. 4:13).

"Humble yourselves, therefore, under God's mighty hand, that he may lift you up in due time. Cast all your anxiety on him because he cares for you" (1 Peter 5:6-7, NIV).

Clean Out the Storage Room

God already knows what's within every dark room in our hearts. He knocks and then waits. We can invite God into the midst of our heavy, painful, and messy burdens.

Think about that packed-to-the-brim storage area in your home. How can it be cleaned thoroughly without pulling everything out to sort and organize it? You know when you start the cleaning-up process that things are going to get a lot messier until the junk is thrown out and the rest is organized.

It's the same with your heart. In the midst of cleaning out the burdens, the mess seems worse. As we start healing emotionally, we often stop the process, because it seems confusing. We don't want to tolerate the messy stage of cleaning out, so we throw our burdens back into the closet. It's important to keep our emotions out in the light until God takes away the junk. This is often not instant; it involves waiting on the Lord as He cleans out that stronghold.

Fear of facing emotions can block the way to freedom. Emotions may hurt you intensely, but they won't kill you. Sometimes, though, as people experience strong emotions, they could conceivably hurt themselves if they don't understand they are actually in the healing process. If you feel like hurting yourself, you must immediately contact professionals to help you.

To enjoy freedom we must begin to look at our emotions in a different way. Strangely, intense sadness or anger can be good, because as those emotions surface, we can let go of them. It's often noticed that emotions seem to gain intensity just before they're released forever. But God will safely carry you through doors of pain as you rest in Him.

When you aren't sure of what to do next, just stop and ask God. Then trust Him to guide you.

"I [the Lord] will instruct you and teach you in the way you should go; I will counsel you with My eye upon you. Be not like the horse or the mule, which lack understanding, which must have their mouths held firm with bit and bridle, or else they will not come with you. Many are the sorrows of the wicked, but he who trusts in, relies on, and confidently leans on the Lord shall be compassed about with mercy and lovingkindness" (Ps. 32:8-10).

When you stop being numb and start feeling and releasing your burdens, you may feel awful for a little while, but then you'll break through. Afterward, you may understand issues you didn't understand before. When your heart room is clean, you can see where everything belongs.

Dump Your Burdens—Don't Haul Them

When you recognize a negative emotional pattern, use this recognition as a handle to take hold of that burden, and then pull it into the light. Thoroughly express the emotion to God, and keep your heart open until you're free. This may mean allowing yourself to experience the feeling—while controlling your behavior—instead of remaining numb. Sometimes God will free you quickly, and other times it may take longer.

It's wise to take a break from the healing process to enjoy life. But don't completely close the door and go back to your old ways of coping.

One of the nicest things you can do for yourself is to become an expert at releasing burdens. It's really a personal choice whether to cope with burdens or dump them. There are many nifty processes you can use to cope with burdens, but it's much better to free yourself from them.

Don't let a miserable feeling hang around for two weeks. Vent in safe ways, have a good cry, and put it behind you. It's far better to feel sad, cry, and get it out of your system than it is to still be carrying the pain 10 years later.

When you're devastated, such as when you lose a loved one, you must grieve. That sort of loss results in an intense, long-lasting grief process. Patience with the process can actually help you let go of the pain. It will take some time, but the beloved one you lost would not want you to grieve forever. Emotional freedom is always possible by God's grace.

You've probably heard that we use only a small percentage of our brainpower. I believe part of the reason for that may be because so much of our minds and hearts are burdened and unavailable for creative problem-solving. A computer file totally full of data can't receive new information until old data is deleted. To effectively use burdened areas of our minds and hearts, the burdens must be deleted. Then we will be receptive to truth and healthy emotions. After these areas are cleansed and healed, meditating on God's Word will renew our thought patterns.

Avoid Taking on Heavy Burdens

Jesus said, "If you abide in My Word [hold fast to My teachings and live in accordance with them], you are truly My disciples. And you will know the Truth, and the Truth will set you free" (John 8:31-32).

Sarah made good progress, but she still felt anxious or sad occasionally. Sarah read the paper and watched the news every day. Being informed has some value, but she was overwhelmed.

When Sarah cut down exposure to bad news, her mood lifted even more. She realized that God did not need her help to run the world, and her worry didn't accomplish anything. When she did watch the news, she prayed for world issues and hurting people and traded her worries for God's peace.

Sarah took more time to read God's Word, and she joined a Bible study. "I will walk about in freedom, for I have sought out your precepts" (Ps. 119:45, NIV). Sarah, as well as other clients I've worked with, decreased sadness and anxiety by focusing on God's goodness and limiting negative exposure.

God and His angels are just as real as crime, terrorism, and war. God's love and power bring hope. "For with God nothing is ever impossible and no word from God shall be without power or impossible of fulfillment" (Luke 1:37).

The evening news, with its incessant review of the world's horrifying events, presents an unbalanced view of reality. Reality is not all negative. Horror, cruelty, and demons exist, but transforming healing, restoration, and grace are available.

Shine God's truth into your problems; meditate on His promises, and pray with faith. Overwhelm negatives with positives. When we're close to God, it's hard to take on burdens, because He's there to carry them. "In my anguish I cried to the LORD, and he answered by setting me free" (Ps. 118:5, NIV).

We can trust God and face our emotions with His help. We can be alive in the moment instead of living a passionless existence. We can release the day-to-day pain of the world into God's hands. He'll give us joy in exchange for our burdens.

Defeating Satan

"We are not wrestling with flesh and blood [contending only with physical opponents], but against the despotisms, against the powers, against [the master spirits who are] the world rulers of this present darkness, against the spirit forces of wickedness in the heavenly (supernatural) sphere" (Eph. 6:12).

"'In your anger do not sin.' Do not let the sun go down while you are still angry, and do not give the devil a foothold" (Eph. 4:26-27).

Let God cleanse you of negative emotions every day. If you don't continually release anger, hurt, and fear, these emotions can build and become footholds or strongholds of the enemy.

The devil does not possess Christians, but he's aware of our weak spots, and his strategy is to jab at us in those weak spots. As you attempt to get free, Satan will try to discourage you. He tries to convince us that no one cares and that escape is hopeless. But you don't need to fear him or listen to his lies. As God's child, you have authority over Satan when you use Jesus' name.

As your heart heals, renounce Satan in Jesus' name, and close any doors that may be open to his evil work. As God cleans out your heart, He'll also push away negative spiritual influence.

Always keep in mind that this is a spiritual battle. The enemy opposes any moves toward freedom and will fight to discourage you. Christians have awe-inspiring weapons to defeat him.

"The weapons we fight with are not weapons of the world. On the contrary, they have divine power to demolish strongholds" (2 Cor. 10:4, NIV).

You'll find the way out when you keep your heart open to Jesus, submit to God, and resist the devil. Plead the blood of Jesus for protection, renounce and reject Satan, and command him to leave in Jesus' name.

I recommended the book *Bondage Breaker,* by Neil Anderson, to Sarah, especially a chapter detailing specific prayers to renounce and close doors to the enemy. Praise also crumbles strongholds.

Praise Your Way Out!

"About midnight, as Paul and Silas were praying and singing hymns of praise to God, and the (other) prisoners were listening to them, Suddenly there was a great earthquake, so that the very foundations of the prison were shaken; and at once all the doors were opened and everyone's shackles were unfastened" (Acts 16:25-26).

When we praise the Lord in every circumstance, He lifts us above the turmoil of life to His kingdom of freedom. Music and praise are powerful burden-lifters. Let your burdens be carried away on a river of praise.

When Joshua defeated the stronghold of Jericho, his battle plan was to seek God's guidance first. God told him to put the choir in front of the army. Under God's direction, they sang, praised Him, and walked around the city until the walls collapsed. Joshua's army was powerless to penetrate the fortress. Angel troops must have demolished the walls with battering rams. Then Joshua's army marched in and conquered the city. God's militia did it for them.

Praise opens the gates for God to rescue you. "He brought them out of darkness and the shadow of death and broke apart the bonds that held them. Oh, that men would praise [and confess to] the Lord His goodness and loving-kindness and His wonderful works to the children of men!" (Ps. 107:14-15).

Continually Releasing Burdens

If we confess our burdens, trust God, and ask Him to release us, He will. God will sometimes bring to our minds more old memories linked to this burden so that old burdens can be released to Him as well.

Walk in the light you have now. As God heals us, He'll reveal more burdens from the past. Then we can become more efficient at dumping burdens every day.

Strongholds or burdens can be small or large. God delivered me from a small stronghold of being late most of the time. I wasn't aware that I harbored resentment toward bossy people and that my schedule was too hectic. When I journaled the emotions that fueled this problem and recognized how bad my attitude was, it was easy to confess it and accept God's healing and deliverance. God granted me freedom from this stronghold with one prayer. I'm usually on time or early now.

Strongholds can be so large that they prevent people from functioning normally. These are accumulations of many heavy burdens that may need to be released a little at a time.

Be honest about all your emotions, including irritation, despair, rage, panic, lust, temptation, or grief. Keep your heart open to God.

Praying with an open heart will propel you toward spiritual and emotional freedom whether your stronghold is too much reliance on caffeine or if it's something as serious as depression or alcoholism. The important thing is to refuse to give up.

Emotional recovery does not need to be a miserable process. It's important to pace yourself and alternate soul-searching with fun activities. Take time to enjoy the good things God has given you. On the worst days there's joy to be found if we expect it.

God lets us enjoy peace and relief for a while after we let go of a major burden. Then when we're ready, He'll make us aware of another burden we carry so we can release it also. Every time we release a burden to God, our hearts become lighter, and life becomes easier and more joyful.

When we understand how to release our burdens and realize how much relief we feel afterward, then the process becomes exciting, even though it's still painful at times. We experience more freedom every time we trust God enough to place our painful burdens into His hands.

God wants to free us from strongholds, remove heavy burdens, and heal our memories. In heaven there will be no more tears. Our final destination is joy.

Checklist to Let God Carry Your Burdens

1. Are you afraid to talk to God when you have a bad or monstrous attitude?
2. Will you let Him touch you where it hurts the most and where you carry the most shame?
3. Will you let your monstrous streak talk to God, even though you know you have a bad attitude? Remember—it's for the purpose of honesty and allowing God to cleanse and heal you, not to justify the bad attitude.
4. Are you afraid God won't forgive and accept you? Even when Jesus died on the Cross because of people's attitudes and actions, He forgave. His mercy is so great that we can't understand it completely.
5. Are you afraid of feeling emotions? Which emotions scare you the most?
6. Can you experience strong emotions and still control your behavior? (If not, wait until you have enough support to tackle those burdens.)
7. Do you think God is big enough to help you with those emotions?
8. Are you willing to get support from mature friends or professionals if needed?
9. Did you pick up any burdens today? This week? This month?
10. Are you willing to give them to God?
11. Do you believe the One who created your heart's emotions can also heal them?
12. Are you willing to walk with God and continually confess your heart truths to Him?

Prayer for Deliverance from Burden Strongholds

God, nothing is impossible for You. You're not limited in any way by my circumstances. I open my heart to You in honesty. I give You my emotional burdens in exchange for Your freedom. I admit that I was born in sin, just like everyone else on this planet. I'm sorry I hurt You by turning away from You. I believe You sent Your Son, Jesus, to be the Savior of this world by dying and paying for our sins and for our emotional freedom.

I'm helpless to overcome this stronghold. I've tried to handle this problem on my own, and it's not working. I open up my heart to You; show me how to pour out my anger, hurt, and fear into Your faithful hands. [Express your true, underlying emotions. If you're angry with God, talk to Him about it.] *Forgive me for holding on to this pain; I didn't realize what I was doing. Clean this poison from my soul.*

Thank You, Jesus, for carrying my sorrows and taking all my burdens upon yourself when You died on the Cross. I accept You, Jesus, as my Savior and Lord right in the middle of this stronghold. I will honor and obey You. I accept Your total forgiveness of my sins. I place all my heavy burdens upon Your broad shoulders.

I praise You and thank You for Your great mercy and compassion. I will continue to trust in You and keep this door to my heart open by being emotionally honest with You. I will wait on You and resist Satan. I rebuke and renounce Satan and all his workers and shut the door to Satan forever in Jesus' name.

Father, give me Your wisdom to handle these situations and grace to forgive those who hurt me. I trust in You, God, to pick me up and carry me out of this stronghold. Thank You for loving me beyond my comprehension. In Jesus' mighty name I pray all these things. Amen.

8

Faith in Action
Walk It Out

As I write in my study today, worship music is playing, and a pine-scented candle is burning. This morning as I prayed for direction, I felt led to share some of my personal journey.

God's grace has carried me through many heartaches and victories. The more I depend on the Lord, the more I enjoy life and experience breakthroughs. I still have struggles, but I run to God with them. When He shows me an area of my life in which I'm relying too much on my own self-sufficiency, I confess it, trust Him, accept His help, and find more freedom as I go.

God freed me from frustration, confusion, and pain in surrendered areas. In the past, it was almost impossible for me to write anything for others to read because of mental blocks or burdens of perfectionism. It was painful for me to write. God delivered me, and now I find joy in writing. God can do the impossible as I trust and lean confidently upon Him.

Breaking Free from Depression

"He heals the brokenhearted and binds up their wounds [curing their pains and their sorrows]" (Ps. 147:3).

Sarah's depression was lifting. She experienced more joy and made a point of having fun with her family nearly every day. Depression is frozen grief. In the past, instead of grieving and letting go of disappointments, Sarah unintentionally held on to her hurts.

Grief is never enjoyable. Grief is a healthful process we must all go through in order to let go of the people and things we love. However, if we get stuck in grief, as Sarah did, we may suffer for the rest of our lives.

Life is full of letting go; time brings one loss after another. The only way out of grief is through it. I wish there were another way. Although we can't avoid facing grief, we can become skillful in working our way through to freedom.

Jesus died to save us from grieving forever. When we fight with grief and attempt to avoid it, we remain captive. When we fully trust God, we can bring all our grief to Him and allow Him to carry us through the door to freedom.

Before seeing me, Sarah trained herself not to cry by telling herself over and over, "Don't cry." Eventually, she wasn't able to cry even when she wanted to.

Sarah corrected this by telling herself repeatedly "It's OK to cry if I need to." She also told herself she wanted to cry only when she was in the privacy of her own home. When her mind was convinced, she was able to cry again.

Healthful crying brings healing and relief, and it's sensible to respect our emotions and acknowledge them as a normal reaction to loss. When we allow ourselves to feel sadness or anger and keep bringing those feelings to God, then we'll be able to release them.

It's damaging to fight sorrowful emotions until they overflow and get to the point where crying can't be controlled. The person may think, *What's wrong with me? I can't stand this anymore. I must be crazy*, creating more emotional damage.

Sarah learned to grieve in healthful ways. She journaled her true emotions, cried, released her burdens, forgave, accepted God's love and grace, and let joy fill her heart.

Breaking Free from Hopelessness

Another client I worked with, Anna, was the victim of childhood incest and carried many heavy burdens. Overwhelmed and suicidal, she lost count over the years of how many times she was hospitalized for her own protection. Her in-patient stays became more and more frequent. When I met her, she had lost custody of her children and was just one step ahead of homelessness.

Anna barely stayed afloat. Like an overloaded boat, her burdens were too heavy. If in counseling we worked too aggressively on her issues, her boat could become unbalanced and sink. So we worked on letting God take small burdens off many areas of her life. When her boat was riding higher above the waves and storms of life, she was ready to more aggressively dump her burdens.

For more than two years, Anna has stayed out of the hospital. Joy is returning, and she's making rapid progress in letting go of her remaining burdens. She recently joined a church, and good friends are pouring love into her life. She's learning to trust her Burden-bearer.

Breaking Free from Addiction

Jenny was an alcoholic. She hated herself for drinking, and she verbally beat on herself after every drinking binge.

Jenny's husband threatened to leave her after she lost her job. She told her husband how sorry she was and tried again and again to stay sober. But she was unable to break the addiction.

When Jenny was tempted to drink, she never felt like praying. She came from a Christian family and accepted Jesus when she was 12; however, she had difficulty trusting God.

Jenny was afraid God would be too angry to listen to her when she was feeling tempted to drink. She admitted that when she felt like drinking she didn't care what God or anyone else thought about it. I asked Jenny to be honest about this with God, especially when she wanted to drink.

She started praying when she was strongly tempted. She admitted to God exactly how she felt right at that moment. She told me that at first she was so angry with God that she was afraid He would strike her with lightning. But God was not shocked—He knew those emotions had festered in Jenny's heart for years.

We sometimes have distorted ideas of who God is. When we're angry with Him, it's because we don't understand Him. When we confess our feelings, God can clear out our incorrect ideas so that we get a clearer picture of who He truly is.

Jenny shut down a part of her mind and emotions that suffered—that's why she didn't want to pray when she felt like drinking. She denied the feelings and drowned them with alcohol. But she could not free herself no matter how hard she tried. She was trying to cut off a God-created place in her heart. Her wounded heart needed cleansing and healing, not self-condemnation.

When she hated herself and tried to push the emotions away, she just pushed poison back into her heart. She was not capable of cleaning out the poison herself, but God could—and did.

Jenny finally admitted that she was powerless against the urge to drink. She decided to fully trust God, accepted the free gift of forgiveness, and accepted Jesus' rescue. The urge to drink became less and less powerful, and eventually she was totally free.

Jenny's Christian boss was kind enough to give her another chance, and her husband stayed. God's grace turns things around.

Breaking Free from Fear

Paula, a young Christian actress, came to talk with me because of panic attacks she had suffered since surviving a life-threatening trauma.

She worked at a technical job and was miserable. Her creative personality was stifled, and she could no longer act because she feared a panic attack would occur while she performed.

Paula rededicated her life to the Lord but felt she was getting nowhere fast. She needed to learn to look to the Lord in the midst of her anxieties and release those fears to Him. Fear is a burden that can be released to God just like any other emotion.

Anxiety and fear can be slippery emotions to get a handle on because we are afraid of fear even more than we're afraid of sadness or anger. It's very easy to keep avoiding fear. However, avoiding the emotion produced by a traumatic memory is actually one of the symptoms of post-traumatic stress disorder. When we continually avoid an emotion, we don't allow God to remove it, and we bear our own burden.

It takes courage to admit and face our fears, but it's necessary to open that door to the heart. It can feel like jumping off a cliff. But God is faithful to carry us through.

Confessing the fear within us and allowing God to free us is the way out. Feeling the fear can take us through a painful door to freedom. We'll find the way out as we trust God to guide us.

Usually, beneath fear is hurt or sadness. The fear is actually a fear of being hurt again. Often when a person gets through the fear, he or she will feel like crying until the root of the fear is cleared out.

The only wholesome fear is the fear or reverence of God. Any other anxiety, fear, or panic needs to be brought directly to God in prayer. As we confess these unhealthful fears of people or circumstances, God will help us forgive others and cleanse us from fear.

It's important to resist the temptation to obsess about our fears rather than to vent our feelings and trust God to deliver us.

Paula learned that God loved even the wounded and fearful parts of her heart. We voiced the details of her frightening experience in prayer and invited God into the memories.

Paula took some small acting jobs and trusted God when she felt anxiety. She talked about finding steady work as an actress. One day I felt led to say, "You have so much talent you could use for God's glory. Let's pray and believe that God will give you a great acting job."

The next day Paula called and excitedly told me she was invited to join a Christian actors' touring group. She left the next week. In correspondence, she said she's doing well and recently married a wonderful Christian man.

Freedom from Rage

Rhonda was a successful businesswoman. She was also an addict. Oh, it was legal. Her addiction combined prescription drugs with a little too much to drink each night. She came to see me after her husband moved out of the house. The precipitating factor was a rage Rhonda expressed one day by breaking several household items.

Rhonda hated her anger. She was ashamed of her behavior, but she didn't know how to change. She felt powerless in the grip of her anger. The people with the most trouble controlling anger actually despise their anger. They may appear to be the calmest, nicest people imaginable, because they disown and dissociate their anger.

Often people with severe anger problems seem to have two parts to their personalities. One part is pleasant, but the other may be out of control and almost impossible to reason with. This emotional split is actually common. You may be married to someone who reacts differently at home than with others. It isn't unusual for someone with a wonderful public personality to be irritable, critical, or unfairly angry with family members. This does not mean the person has multiple personality disorder or is schizophrenic. The emotional pain buried partly in the subconscious mind can be triggered by various things.

Even quiet, gentle personalities can be passive aggressive, sarcastic, or verbally destructive. We're responsible for our words, attitudes, and actions, no matter how others treat us. Jesus forgave others even as they crucified Him. It would be foolish to needlessly expose ourselves to abuse. However, if we encounter abuse, Jesus is the example for our response. We can put ourselves under God's control and learn to express anger in healthful ways that are not destructive.

Rhonda learned that anger can be used in positive ways. Anger gives strength to fight wrongs. Communicating our anger in a respectful or loving way is often the only means of setting healthful boundaries with others. It's never OK to express anger in hate. "Let everything you do be done in love (true love to God and man as inspired by God's love for us)" (1 Cor. 16:14). This includes expressing anger in love. If you can't talk without a harsh or sarcastic tone, don't talk. Anger is positive only if used for the good of others.

What can you do if you feel swept along by a powerful rage? What can you do when you feel the situation is hopeless?

Pray. Nothing else will get you through without harm. Look to God in the midst of the emotional storm. Wait for Him; trust Him, and He'll help you. Stop trying to handle anger on your own. Make a conscious decision to release it to God instead of lashing out. Plan to run to God the next time you're angry. Instead of damaging yourself or others with rage, let God carry you until you're free.

"Contend, O LORD, with those who contend with me; fight against those who fight against me. Take up shield and buckler; arise and come to my aid. Brandish spear and javelin against those who pursue me. Say to my soul, 'I am your salvation.'

"May those who seek my life be disgraced and put to shame; may those who plot my ruin be turned back in dismay. May they be like chaff before the wind, with the angel of the LORD driving them away; may their path be dark and slippery, with the angel of the LORD pursuing them" (Ps. 35:1-6, NIV).

Notice in the above passage that David didn't take revenge into his own hands. He poured out his complaint and let God take care of his enemies. Journaling what your anger would say if it could scream is one way to get in touch with rage during quieter moments. The best time to journal your anger is when you feel angry, because the feelings are surfacing then. Your anger is coming out into the light. When you're furious, agitated, or annoyed, that's the most opportune time to let God grab hold of the roots of your anger and pull it out.

Do you think King David felt perfectly calm when he asked God to destroy his enemies? David went directly to God with his rage and found God's peace and direction. Just because we feel extreme anger doesn't mean we must act it out. We can separate our behavior from our emotions with God's help.

It's important that we not unleash our anger onto our loved ones. However, when we're alone with God, we can expose our anger to the light of His truth and let it all out. If we can't find the words, we can yell or cry until we release that burden. As we trust God with the process, we'll be set free. God will hear when we speak from our hearts, and He'll forgive, clear out the anger, and deliver us.

As Rhonda continually invited Jesus into the middle of her anger and released her burdens to Him, she gradually became healed and free. Her husband returned home once he felt assured she could control her temper.

"The eternal God is your refuge and dwelling place, and underneath are the everlasting arms" (Deut. 33:27).

Christian Maturity

"Do not be conformed to this world (this age) [fashioned after and adapted to its external, superficial customs], but be transformed (changed) by the [entire] renewal of your mind [by its new ideals and its new attitude] so that you may prove [for yourselves] what is the good and acceptable and perfect will of God" (Rom. 12:2).

In the preceding verse "mind" in the Greek means intellect, which includes our thoughts, *feelings*, or will.[1]

Christian maturity includes learning to trust God completely, no matter what happens. Maturity in this world means becoming more self-sufficient, but growing in Christian strength and maturity means leaning more and more on God.

Many people stop growing and have no idea of how to get unstuck. It's important to evaluate on a regular basis where we're heading. Ask God if you're following Him. To win the race, we must make right decisions each day. Life is a process of loss and growth, change and movement. If we stop making progress, it's usually because of heavy burdens.

One may struggle with burdens of anger, another with depression or fear. If you encounter a familiar struggle, don't be discouraged. Just become aware of the next burden to release. Remind yourself of past God-given victories, and keep going!

I asked God to show me if there was a way to set a person free all at once. I feel that He showed me that the process of seeing what's truly in our hearts can be painful, but that's always the first step. While God can set us free in powerful ways, it's usually just one burden at a time.

The process of handling emotions according to spiritual principles is a lifelong journey. It's one thing to become free and another to stay free. Once we've experienced freedom, we must continue to use truth to remain free. No magic answers exist for emotional wholeness. If you try these keys and discard them, you won't experience true freedom. But if you take time to prayerfully integrate scriptural principles into your life, God will change you.

As we keep our eyes on Jesus and continually cast our cares upon Him, we're released daily from old and new burdens. We can become efficient at letting go of past hurts, present frustrations, and worries about the future.

It helps to have a quiet time every day with the Lord, reading His Word, and prayerfully placing each burden into His hands. You'll have the freedom to realize your full potential as God removes the sludge of emotional burdens.

Nothing compares to the wisdom we find in reading and studying God's Word, which shines a light on the emotional and spiritual dimensions of our lives and shows us how to let God carry us through. Humble dependence on God is true Christian maturity.

God transforms us into the image of Christ (see Rom. 8:29). We're refined as gold in the furnace is refined to remove impurities. Life pressures force burdens to the surface so they can be removed. As God purifies the depths of our hearts, gold is revealed, and joy surfaces.

God releases us, protects us from taking on heavy burdens, and gives us faith to stay emotionally free. "Whatever is born of God is victorious over the world; and this is the victory that conquers the world, even our faith" (1 John 5:4).

Avoid Unnecessary Burdens

"Come to me, all you who are weary and burdened, and I will give you rest. Take my yoke upon you and learn from me, for I am gentle and humble of heart, and you will find rest for your souls. For my yoke is easy and my burden is light" (Matt. 11:28-30, NIV).

When Jesus pulls the yoke with us, His strength and ability make the way easier. When we feel overburdened, we can let Him take on the extra weight. "Looking away [from all that will distract] to Jesus, Who is the Leader and the Source of our faith [giving the first incentive for our belief] and is also its Finisher [bringing it to maturity and perfection]" (Heb. 12:2). If we focus on Jesus and depend on His strength, He'll give us grace to overcome.

Although we must deal with harsh realities, if we put those negatives under a magnifying glass, they'll grow until they block out the positives. The world is full of opportunities to become burdened. If we aren't careful, we'll collect new burdens every day. It's better not to take burdens on in the first place.

To stay emotionally free, avoid evil and limit frightening input from books, music, and media. If you try to digest emotional and spiritual poison, it will burden you and can lead to anxiety, depression, and addictions. Don't be slimed by the world—be cleansed by the Word. The Word brings life, but exposure to sin leads to emotional and physical sickness and death.

Keep your mind on God and the wonderful aspects of life. Take advantage of the vast quantities of uplifting Christian books, magazines, music, and radio and television programs.

Pour more positives than negatives into your heart and mind, and unexpected joy will erupt.

"Whatever is true, whatever is worthy of reverence and is honorable and seemly, whatever is just, whatever is pure, whatever is lovely and lovable, whatever is kind and winsome and gracious, if there is any virtue and excellence, if there is anything worthy of praise, think on and weigh and take account of these things [fix your minds on them]" (Phil. 4:8).

God enables us to overcome the world by faith. Our overriding hope and trust is that God is in charge. We're completely victorious when Jesus is our personal Savior.

The way to true peace and joy is to focus on God and reflect His light and love into our surroundings. We can have peace and joy in spite of troubles because of who we trust. We need only to carry a light load of obedience and trust. We stay free by transferring our burdens to Jesus' broad shoulders every day.

Claiming Our Freedom by Faith

"We walk by faith [we regulate our lives and conduct ourselves by our conviction or belief respecting man's relationship to God and divine things, with trust and holy fervor; thus we walk] not by sight or appearance" (2 Cor. 5:7).

Pinpoint the strong emotion or burden you struggle with most, whether it's fear, anger, obsession, or sadness. Let that suffering part of your heart cry out to God for deliverance.

Don't try to work yourself up emotionally, but don't be afraid to pray with all your heart as you let God free you. Cry out to God from the midst of the emotions as you release burdens.

"Save me O God; for the waters have come up to my neck [they threaten my life]. I sink in deep mire, where there is no foothold; I have come into deep waters, where the floods overwhelm me. I am weary with my crying; my throat is parched; my eyes fail with waiting [hopefully] for my God. . . ."

"Hide not Your face from Your servant, for I am in distress. O answer me speedily! . . ."

"I am poor, sorrowful, and in pain; let Your salvation, O God, set me up on high. I will praise the name of God with a song and will magnify him with thanksgiving. . . ."

"For the Lord hears the poor and needy and despises not His prisoners (His miserable and wounded ones). Let heaven and earth praise Him, the seas and everything that moves in them. For God will save" (Ps. 69:1-3, 17, 29-30, 33-35).

King David in this psalm demonstrates the way to give God our burdens and how to be delivered from strongholds. (See also Ps. 6:6-10; 38:8-22; 102:20).

David knew the way to freedom. No matter what he faced, he knew he could always come to God. In honesty, he opened his heart before God and poured out the emotional burden he was suffering. After he confessed exactly what was in his heart, he waited upon the Lord for salvation.

This prayer doesn't always need to be extremely emotional to be powerful. The important thing is to trust God with each piece of our hearts and admit whatever burden it carries. Our hearts can speak directly to God.

"Then they cried to the Lord in their trouble, and He delivered them out of their distresses" (Ps. 107:13).

"Truly, I say to you, if you have faith [that is living] as a grain of mustard seed, you can say to this mountain, Move from here to yonder place, and it will move; and nothing will be impossible to you" (Matt. 17:20).

Simply breaking out of a stronghold is not enough; we must allow Jesus to fill the void the burdens leave behind. We'll stay free as we meditate on God's Word, obey Him, and stay close to other believers.

Checklist for Continual Deliverance

1. Have you had any fun this week? (It isn't good for you to focus only on problems.)
2. Do you immediately talk to God about any bad attitudes and let Him help you?
3. Are you starting to talk to God about your persistent attitudes, emotions, and behaviors as you become aware of them? If not, why not?
4. What's the hardest emotion for you to bring to God—sadness, fear, or anger?
5. Do you trust God with your happiness as well?

6. Do you try to clean up your thoughts and feelings on your own?
7. Do you realize that all your abilities are God-given gifts? Do you seek to constantly depend on Him, or do you depend on your own knowledge and abilities?
8. Do you ingest emotional and spiritual poison from the media?
9. Do you realize you need God's guidance and read God's Word on a regular basis?
10. Is God-dependence your heart attitude? Do you pray often?
11. Do you focus more on how much God loves and cares for you or on your problems?
12. Do you realize that Jesus wants to live in your heart as your closest friend and is intensely interested in helping you with each struggle?

Prayer for Continual Deliverance

Lord, You're more than sufficient for all my needs. I come to You and humbly confess that I can't remove this burden in my own strength. Even though I already trusted You for salvation, I realize that this part of me hasn't fully trusted You yet. Forgive me, Lord. I invite Jesus to be my Savior in this area as well.

I renounce Satan and forbid him to bother me anymore. In the glorious name of Jesus I claim my freedom. I plead the blood of Jesus over this part of my life forever.

Lord, I open this door of my heart to Your light and love. Thank You for making it possible for me to roll my burdens onto Your broad shoulders. Carry me, Lord; forgive me for doing things my own way.

I will wait on You for Your peace and guidance. I will not act on my own thoughts and emotions in this area anymore. I will wait until I have clear direction from You. Enable me to forgive those who hurt me.

Take this wounded, burdened piece of my heart and mind; cleanse, heal, and mend it. Bind my heart back together, Lord; make me whole again. Father God, I thank You by faith for releasing, healing, and setting me free. I command these burdens be gone forever in the powerful name of Jesus.

"Teach me Your way, O Lord, that I may walk and live in Your

truth; direct and unite my heart [solely, reverently] to fear and honor Your name. I will confess and praise You, O Lord my God, with my whole (united) heart; and I will glorify Your name forevermore" [Ps. 86:11-12].

Father, I praise You for Your wisdom. You live in total light; nothing is hidden from You. Grant me wisdom to be as wise as a serpent and as harmless as a dove. Open my eyes to avoid unnecessary burdens. Guide me each day to release all my burdens to You. I will trust You to carry me. You will give me the ability and knowledge I need to address each situation successfully. I will wait for Your guidance. Thank You for the good You're accomplishing in my life. I pray this in the all-sufficient name of Jesus. Amen.

Prayer to Release Burdens of Sadness or Depression

God, I praise You for Your tender heart; You promised to be close to the brokenhearted. I confess right now that I'm suffering. I'm having trouble trusting You. Forgive me for trying to handle this on my own. I pour this sadness out to You. Take this specific burden away forever. [Tell God everything that's hurting you.] *Heal my wounded heart. Fill me with Your comfort. I accept Jesus as my Savior and Lord, to mend my heart and deliver me from this grief. I put my trust in You for the situation I'm sad about. I put my faith in You, that You'll heal and deliver me. Come into this dark room in my heart; bring Your light and love. I will wait for You. I pray this in the powerful name of Jesus. Amen.*

Prayer to Release Burdens of Anxiety or Fear

Father, I praise You that nothing is too hard for You. Compared to You, my fear [or worry] *is only a tiny problem. I confess I've tried to handle this fear on my own. I've had trouble trusting You. You promised to forgive and cleanse me from all unrighteousness. Forgive me for hating myself for being afraid. I bring this hurting, fearful part of my heart to You. I believe You'll forgive me, take this burden of fear from me, and heal my heart.*

Give me courage to feel and confess the fear inside. [Let the fearful part of your heart talk to God. Explain to God all the details of your fears.] *I pour all the fear out to You and ask You to remove this burden from my heart. I put my trust in Jesus Christ, the Savior of the world, to save me from my fears. I invite You to come into the middle of my fear. Bring Your light and love and rescue me! I wait on Your salvation. I wait on Your direction. I bind Satan in the name of Jesus so that he cannot attack me in this area any longer. I reject and renounce the spirit of fear forever in Jesus' name. I praise You, God, that You will totally set me free. I pray this in the wonderful name of Jesus. Amen.*

Prayer to Release Burdens of Anger or Rage

Father God, I confess that I'm furious. All I want to do is dump this anger on someone. I praise You that You're able to help me right now. I confess that I can't handle this on my own. Although I'm very angry right now, I'm not talking to You about this to be disrespectful. I'm bringing my anger to You to confess it and let You free me from it.

I confess that I'm hurting. I confess to You exactly what I feel and think right now. [Let the angry part of your heart talk to God. Take some time to talk (or yell) to God about your troubles.]

I trust in You to heal me and handle this situation for me. I confess that the way I usually handle my anger is wrong and destructive. It hasn't accomplished anything positive. My anger has damaged my relationships and me. Forgive me, Lord. Cleanse me from unrighteousness. Give me Your love for others so that I'll no longer damage them with my anger. I invite You into the middle of my anger right now. Take this burden of anger off me.

I rebuke and renounce Satan and his workers. I shut the door on them forever. I forbid them to cause any more damage in this area any longer, in Jesus' name.

Father God, I won't do anything until You give me clear direction. I would rather feel as if I might explode from the force of this anger [you won't] *than hurt the ones I love. Strengthen me to do what's right. I'm waiting and holding on to You, Lord. I'll wait until You give me peace about what I should do. I trust that You're here and that You'll answer and guide me. Thank You for listening to me. I believe You'll carry me through this. I pray all this in the mighty name of Jesus. Amen.*

PART 3

Keys to Freedom in Relationships

Reach into My Heart

I praise You, God our Father, who lives in holy light.
Your right hand is exalted with power and with might.
Reach into my heart, Lord, as I say this prayer.
Shine Your light upon me; show me what is there.

See if there is any painful or wicked way in me.
Light the path before me, set me completely free.
Reach into my life, Lord, with Your caring hand.
Heal my hurting places, and help me understand.

You alone can carry my burdens and my cares.
I open up my heart; I know that You are there.
Reach into my life, Lord, my mind, heart, and soul;
Search all that is within me—I give You full control.

Search me with Your candle till all the darkness shines.
Your truth will set me free from all of sin's designs.
Reach into my heart, Lord. Put compassion there
For the needs of others; their sorrows I will share.

Together we will come to You, the only source of love.
Your love alone can heal us, Holy Father from above.
Remove all our burdens, the sin and guilty shame;
Heal all our brokenness, we pray in Jesus' name.

—Robin Martens

9
Confess
Open the Door

———————

"The fear of man brings a snare, but whoever leans on, trusts and puts his confidence in the Lord is safe and set on high" (Prov. 29:25).

Relationships can be our greatest blessings or our greatest burdens. Sparkling personalities lift our spirits; doomsayers drag us down. To become free, we must take a close look at our relationships.

One of your most important relationships is with yourself. You can be discouraged or encouraged by your self-talk. Living with yourself 24 hours a day can be uplifting or horrible, depending on what's in your heart.

Our relationships with God, others, and ourselves determine how many burdens we carry through life.

Our Relationship with God

God can't fully pour His love into us until we fully open our hearts to Him. "(I always pray) the God of our Lord Jesus Christ, the Father of glory, that He may grant you a spirit of wisdom and revelation [of insight into mysteries and secrets] in the [deep and intimate] knowledge of Him, By having the eyes of your heart flooded with light, so that you can know and understand the hope to which He has called you, and how rich is His glorious inheritance in the saints (His set-apart ones)" (Eph. 1:17-18).

We're on a lifelong journey from total darkness to total light. We're all born as sinners into a dark world. God's purpose is to transform us completely: our spirits, our minds, our hearts, and eventually even our bodies into the image of His Son Jesus—the light of the world.

"Your eye is the lamp of your body; when your eye (your conscience) is sound and fulfilling its office, your whole body is full of light; but when it is not sound and is not fulfilling its office, your body is full of darkness. Be careful, therefore, that the light that is in you is not darkness. If then your entire body is illuminated, having no part dark, it will be wholly bright [with light], as when a lamp with its bright rays gives you light" (Luke 11:34-36).

If we see things only one way, that means our eye is whole and sound. However, when we see things one way with the mind (logically) and another way with the heart (emotionally), we're not yet full of light. If we know God's love with the mind but not the heart, our eyes are not yet whole or sound. We've not been perfected in His love when we're afraid God doesn't love us, because perfect love casts out all fear (1 John 4:18).

God is merciful, and His intentions toward us are loving. One who is mature will have a relationship with God that recognizes His loving discipline as well as His tenderness. Although the Lord forgives us and loves us enough to have died for us, He also disciplines us for our benefit. Furthermore, we may suffer natural consequences when we wander away from God's protection.

"Do not despise or shrink from the chastening of the Lord [His correction by punishment or by subjection to suffering or trial]; neither be weary of or impatient about or loathe or abhor His reproof. For whom the Lord loves He corrects, even as a father corrects the son in whom he delights" (Prov. 3:11-12).

God is usually very gentle with us when we first decide to trust Him. But as we grow as Christians, God disciplines and teaches us so we can be partakers of His nature and heavenly rewards. His discipline is proof of His love.

God's nature is a perfect balance of love and discipline. All healthy relationships are based upon the balance between mercy and judgment, tenderness and righteous anger, as well as generosity and proper boundaries.

Your Relationship with Yourself

"You must love the Lord your God with all your heart, and

with all your soul, and with all your strength, and with all your mind; and your neighbor as yourself" (Luke 10:27).

God wants us to love Him and others; nothing is more important. He has compassion on us and wants us to be compassionate to ourselves as well as to others.

This is different than feeling sorry for yourself. When people are angry with themselves for feeling emotional pain, they may ask themselves, *What's wrong with me? Why am I so upset? I'm sick of feeling this way. This is stupid.* This is injurious and the opposite of simply having some compassion when we hurt, just as we would have compassion for another. Nothing is worse than living with an enemy. We're our own worst enemy when we hate our emotions rather than take care of them with God's help.

We can't have healthy relationships with others until we have good relationships with ourselves. We usually treat the emotions of others the same way we handle our own. If we're kind, understanding, and self-controlled in the way we care for ourselves, we'll treat others compassionately. If we hate ourselves, we won't have patience with others either. It's difficult to be in close relationships if we don't like ourselves.

Martha's work was never done. She cleaned and vacuumed almost every day after work. It didn't matter how she felt—she forced herself to keep up her standards. Her house was always neat, clean, and polished. If not, she or the family was pressed into action.

Martha heard her son's school bus pull up, she heard shouts, and then Jason stormed into the house. She saw that his shoes had left thick clumps of mud on her freshly waxed floor in the entry hall.

Jason was crying as she yelled at him, "Don't you ever think? I'm so tired of you messing up my house! What's wrong with you? Get out of here!" She shoved Jason out the door and locked it behind him. She was so mad about her floor that she couldn't think of anything else. Outside, Jason fumed and contemplated running away.

Martha's friend Mary sat by her picture window and sipped orange tea as she crocheted. Her work was never done, but she took time to relax anyway. Her house was usually neat and clean, but

Mary had a relaxed attitude. She could tolerate some disorder if the needs of family or friends interfered with her cleaning schedule.

She saw the yellow school bus approach slowly and stop. A few children and her daughter Jessica got off the bus. Mary saw right away that she was upset. Before Mary could get to a good place to stop crocheting, Jessica came in and slammed the door. She was crying, and Mary could see that she had tracked in a lot of mud.

"Jessica, what's wrong?"

Jessica told her that a boy on the bus had called her names. When she got off the bus, her friend Jason yelled at him for being a jerk, and then the boy hit Jason in return.

Mary said, "Jessica, take off your shoes, come sit here by me, and tell me about it. How can I help?"

Jessica cried and said, "I'm so angry! How can anyone be so mean! I'm worried about Jason—he was hit hard."

Mary said, "Do you want me to call Jason's mom and see how he's doing?"

"Yes, Mom—that would help."

Mary called Martha and told her what had happened. Martha decided to let Jason back in the house and told Mary that he was fine. Then Mary called the school and reported the incident.

By this time Jessica calmed down and was feeling better.

"Jessica, come and help me clean this floor up."

Mary and Jessica had a good evening, but Martha and Jason barely spoke to each other.

It would emotionally damage children to lock them out of the house every time they make a mistake. But we don't think twice about locking our emotions out of our own hearts. The effect is the same. When we reject emotions, they escalate, but if we care for them properly, they calm down.

If we realize we have abusive self-talk or feel stupid or unlovable, we should confess it to the Lord. It isn't right to be hurtful to ourselves. When we confess that we've been harsh with others or ourselves, God will forgive and cleanse us from that wrong attitude. We must care for our own hearts and the hearts of others to be free.

Your Relationships with Others

"Let everything you do be done in love (true love to God and man as inspired by God's love for us)" (1 Cor. 16:14).

Try to listen to the hearts and emotions of others as well as to their words. One summer our son told us he didn't want to go to the public high school in the fall. He didn't have a logical reason, but we heard and cared about the distress behind his words. After praying, we decided to send him to a Christian school. It was the right decision. The small classes and supportive teachers gave him confidence. He loved it and graduated as valedictorian.

We can't be truly close to others if we never listen to their hearts. We can't make wise relationship decisions without including our hearts and emotions. Even left-brain, analytical people must realize that emotions can be important factors in sound decision-making.

It's impossible to be happy in any relationship without a humble decision to keep loving and forgiving the other person. "By pride and insolence comes only contention, but with the well-advised is skillful and godly Wisdom" (Prov. 13:10).

In disagreements, make a decision to be the first to forgive. To forgive means not only to make a mental decision to forgive, but also a heart decision to release the burdens of hurt and bitterness to God.

We're responsible to obey God regardless of how others behave. When we stand before God, He won't discuss how difficult anyone made it for us. He'll consider our thoughts and our actions. He'll check to see if we overcame by our faith in Him, or if we blamed others for our failures.

It's supremely important to love the Lord your God with all your heart, mind, soul, and strength and your neighbor as yourself. Loving your neighbor includes everyone in your family. It includes the most difficult person you may have to relate to.

How do we truly love others, especially those who hit all our sore spots? It's easy to keep reacting to them with hurt and anger. It's human nature to fire back when we're attacked. We think, *That'll teach them not to treat me that way!* We don't realize we just gave them more ammunition for their next attack. This approach only intensifies conflict and jeopardizes relationships.

We must stop attacking the ones we love, no matter how they behave. We need to protect them from our destructive anger, name-calling, or even a hateful tone of voice. Of course, we would protect our family from harm—from sickness or danger. But do we protect them from abusive words from our own mouths? It's amazing how vicious humans can be, especially with those they love.

God hears whether we speak to our family in love or not. No matter how we're treated ourselves, we're responsible for how we think, act, and react.

Hippocrates wrote that physicians should "help or do not harm."[1] This is also a great guideline for interacting with fellow human beings.

In a verbally or physically damaging relationship, it can be difficult to stop the negative cycle from continuing to spin viciously. The force of emotions can feel overwhelming. Trying to control words and actions in the middle of an argument is like holding on to a pole in a hurricane. We can make a conscious decision to be responsible for our actions and reactions no matter how others treat us. If we don't know what to do, we can look to God and hold on to Him until the storm passes. It's better to do nothing while you wait for God to intervene than to behave in hateful and destructive ways.

If just one person takes responsibility for his or her actions, wonderful things can happen in a relationship. If both take responsibility, amazing healing can spring forth. Wounds start healing, and love has a chance to grow.

It's important to get the poison of old hurts, disappointments, and anger out of our systems. However, it is just as important that we don't dump this misery onto another person. If we're hurt or angry with someone, we need to vent it, but not to the person. We must go to God first and be honest with Him and ourselves about how we feel.

We can write it out as King David did in his psalms—and then throw the paper away. Make sure the other person doesn't see any damaging words. We can yell at the person in our heads without saying anything out loud. The purpose is not to hurt or blame others. It may be that we're overreacting or have a bad attitude. The purpose is to see what's in our hearts and let God forgive us and clean out our bad attitudes.

The only way to clean it out is to bring it into the light, but we must release the pain in safe ways. It's never God's will for us to be hateful or hurtful to anyone. Our goal is always to love and forgive the other person. However, this can't be done by lying to ourselves and pretending we're not hurt and angry when we are. That's like sweeping dirt under the carpet. It doesn't clean up the problem; it only hides it. The dirt must be thrown out the back door without dumping it on anyone.

Only God can help us clean out pain we've accumulated for years. People can support us, but only God can cleanse our hearts. If we dump emotional poison on people, they'll usually withdraw or attack. Most people can't even hear what you're saying if you upset them. The higher the level of emotion, the less we're able to think or solve problems logically.

Confrontation isn't always necessary, and in some cases it can damage relationships. The other person has no magic words to make you feel better anyway—only God can genuinely heal you and lighten your load.

After God takes your burden and gives you wisdom and peace, you may feel led to confront the other person in love. If you don't feel love for the other person and peace about discussing the issue with him or her, you aren't ready. If and when you do attempt to talk through a disagreement, make sure you take responsibility for your own share of the problem.

Take Responsibility

Human nature is to see the faults of others more clearly than our own, but if your relationship has problems, you're a factor. You're half of the relationship and must take your share of responsibility for prayers to be effective. No one can carry us through life except God. It's crucial that we take personal responsibility for our own spiritual and emotional journeys in life. We realize we need to take responsibility for our finances and our physical health, but we don't always realize that we're responsible for our emotional and spiritual health.

We look to our friends or family for answers. Often we're

content to sit back and soak up the pastor's message every Sunday. We hope the church, family, or friends will meet our needs, but we often fail to seek the only wellspring of love and sufficiency—God himself.

We're responsible to love and forgive others no matter how they act toward us. Even though we can't force others to change, we can take responsibility by praying for them and for our relationship. It's powerful to pray together if possible.

"If two of you on earth agree about anything you ask for, it will be done for you by my Father in heaven. For where two or three come together in my name, there am I with them" (Matt. 18:19-20, NIV). If the other person isn't interested in praying with you, don't be discouraged. Heaven will agree with you whenever you pray according to the Father's will.

When you pray about a relationship—with someone else or by yourself—use the words *we*, *our*, and *us*. When you pray together, the other person's defenses will come down when you admit your part of the problem.

As you humble yourself and admit you aren't perfect, God's light will shine on your attitudes. What you see may surprise you—and set you free.

If you aren't happy, it may be that you're not allowing God's love to flow through you. You can't change others with your displeasure, so you might as well focus on the good and enjoy your relationships. Leave it in God's hands to change them. He's the only one with power to change people, so you might as well relax. The only way to keep relationships healthy is entrust them to God's care.

Checklist to Identify Relationship Burdens

1. Do you feel lonely in spite of your relationships?
2. Do you have chronic emotional pain in a relationship? Have you checked with God to see if He wants you in that relationship?
3. Do you suffer from insecurity in relationships?
4. Are you a friend or an enemy to yourself?
5. Are you compassionate with the emotions of others?
6. Are you compassionate with your own heart?

7. Are you drifting apart from someone you love? Are you willing to ask God for courage to address the problem?

8. Does a pattern of boredom, resentment, or worry cause problems in a relationship?

9. Do you have a constant disagreement in a relationship? Does it upset you, or are you both peaceful about it? Can you accept each other in spite of different views?

10. Do you trust God when you're in the middle of a disagreement with someone you love, or do you panic and get out of control with your emotions?

11. Do you have a few close friends you can be yourself with? If not, why not? What issues prevent you from forming close friendships?

12. Are there some emotional issues separating you from healthy relationships? Can you bring them to God for healing?

Prayer to Confess Relationship Burdens

God, we praise You for Your kind and forgiving nature. Thank You for being patient with us. Forgive us for criticizing instead of loving. Forgive us for trying to resolve problems by ourselves rather than asking for help from our Creator.

We admit we can't handle this problem in this relationship. All we've tried has failed. We're turning this problem over to You; help us to stop handling things our own way. We have no idea how You'll solve it, but we know You have the answers. Forgive us for trying to manage this without You. Help us to forgive each other and ourselves. We'll wait for Your guidance. Carry us through this, Lord. In Jesus' name we pray. Amen.

10

Believe

God's Grace Will Transform Relationships

"If we [really] are living and walking in the Light, as He [Himself] is in the Light, we have [true, unbroken] fellowship with one another, and the blood of Jesus Christ His Son cleanses (removes) us from all sin and guilt [keeps us cleansed from sin in all its forms and manifestations]" (1 John 1:7).

Walking in the light of who we are and who God is keeps us free. What does it mean to walk in the light? It means to see as God sees. It means to be unafraid to shine God's light (the truth of His Word) into all the dark crevices of our hearts. It means we bring all our difficult emotions and negative thoughts to God. Knowing that God forgives, accepts, and loves us gives us courage to walk in the light.

When we continually confess all we are and at the same time focus on all God is, then we allow His light, grace, and love to overwhelm our neediness with His provision. We can walk in victory and have close relationships with one another. Faith in God's love, mercy, and grace through what Jesus accomplished on the Cross is a key to freedom in relationships.

Our trust in God must grow for us to be able to walk before Him in total light. We have no need to fear being totally honest and open with God. He wants us to continue to walk in the light of the truth in His Word even when it exposes darkness in our relationships and us. As we continually bring dark areas to God for cleansing, He will free us emotionally.

To release relationship burdens and heal emotional wounds, we need to expose them to God and sometimes to a Christian friend. We can bring our burdens to the light and be freed from them only when we learn to trust God and others.

Freedom is the clarion call Jesus proclaimed from the kingdom of heaven. This emancipation begins as we take God's hand in trust.

Trusting God

Sarah was frustrated today. Her husband, Mike, did not provide the emotional support she needed.

"Isn't it God's will that my husband treat me in a loving way?" she asked.

"Yes," I said, "but we can't *make* another person obey God."

She read many books on how husbands should treat wives, but Mike didn't care what the experts said and didn't respond to her attempts to correct their relationship.

Sarah admitted that nagging didn't work. Instead, she decided to trust God, and she chose to be more loving toward Mike. If he hurt her feelings, she told him in a kind way or even cried, but she quit trying to change him. If Mike started verbally abusing her, she just got up and left the room or told him she was going for a walk and would be back in a little while. She stopped threatening to leave him, but she set loving boundaries and didn't allow him to hurt her and their relationship by being unkind. Sarah learned to continually give her hurt, frustration, and irritation to God instead of dumping it on her husband. As God's love filled and healed her heart, she was able to pass that compassion, love, and joy on. She didn't wait for Mike to deserve her love, but she gave affection freely.

Mike gradually became more careful with her feelings; he stopped threatening and trying to motivate her with verbal abuse. His resistance melted as Sarah became kinder as well as setting firmer boundaries with him. Mike saw God work in Sarah's life and became more open to her suggestions. Together they learned to look to God for guidance, and Sarah was convinced that God's grace was carrying them through each difficulty.

Sarah learned to depend on God's resources and continually released her burdens to God. Prayers started being answered, and their marriage improved. Sarah continued to move forward. She started to lead her Bible study, and her work supervisor commended her improved attitude.

To have mature, loving relationships with people, our relationship with God must be our firm foundation. People will always disappoint us, but God never will. God can be the Rock we stand on. He'll enable us to withstand any life storm or disappointment.

Even if every one else fails us, God will hold us up. God is the source of everything good. Our loved ones are not the source—they're only channels of God's love. We may see the people in our lives as great obstacles to our happiness. When we worry and fret, wishing they would change, we only waste our time.

We tend to think our spouses, our children, our bosses, or our enemies can keep us from accomplishing God's purpose in our lives. But compared to God, they're smaller than ants and just as helpless. God can bless us through them, around them, over them, under them, in spite of them. Trust God, and move forward. God will take care of the people around you when you're committed to doing His will.

The key is to ask God for directions. We need to wait on Him and do what He tells us to do. He can bring good out of any situation and give us power to overcome if we put Him totally in charge.

We struggle when we try to handle our relationships ourselves. To turn problems around, confess that you didn't trust God to act on your behalf. Then stop reacting the same way you have in the past, even if you have no idea how else to handle the situation. When the stress is on, it's often better to do nothing. When we trust God and wait on Him, it's amazing what can happen. Although God is invisible, He has much more power to change our relationships than we do. When we understand and trust His love for us, we have more to give others.

The favor of people rises and falls like ocean waves, but God's love is a forever-enduring rock. We can trust God's love to hold us steady even through the winds of changing human affection.

Trusting Others

We can trust God to love us through others, but only His love is perfect. However, we need to trust for relationships to be healthy. Love, peace, and trust join us; suspicion, hatred, and bitterness divide us.

As God carries us, we'll be strong enough to trust, forgive, and keep our hearts open to our brothers and sisters. As descendants of Adam and Eve, we're all family. As a loving parent, God wants His children to get along. However, we need wisdom to love our imperfect siblings.

It isn't wise to be emotionally transparent with everyone, but we do need to be honest with God, trusted friends or counselors, and ourselves.

Homeless people often don't know whom to trust and are repeatedly victimized. Many homeless women I counseled lost all their possessions several times. People they trusted either left with their things or threw them out. Many had trusted abusers, rapists, and thieves and paid a terrible price.

In less extreme ways, many of us look for someone to take care of us emotionally. We all have a learning curve before we know who is trustworthy. However, the only One who is totally trustworthy and capable of taking care of our emotions is God. God can lead us to caring people, but they'll still let us down—even when they don't mean to. People are limited.

It's emotionally damaging to be treated in a condescending way. If friends act as if they're superior, they're probably not safe. Harsh criticism is destructive even if it contains some truth. Children of God don't have to accept condemnation from anyone. Someone who's condemning or acts superior is not a loving person and should probably be avoided. It's wise to accept constructive criticism, but it's damaging to absorb hate or condemnation. Some Christians and churches are not mature and can be destructive. God is love, and He is perfect. Christians don't act perfect yet.

It's important to discern who is safe and who is not. We need support; we can't do it alone. We're damaged in the context of hurtful relationships, and being in healthy relationships can heal us. A book can't tell us to stop and go over that page again, but a counselor or a trustworthy Christian friend can gently tell us where we need work.

Some people get all the help they need through their friends.

But Christian counseling can be necessary if emotional struggles are severe or if a person doesn't know anyone safe. It's important to find a Christian who's mature and who understands how emotions heal. Love and compassion heal us, along with caring confrontation.

"Confess to one another therefore your faults (your slips, your false steps, your offenses, your sins) and pray [also] for one another, that you may be healed and restored [to a spiritual tone of mind and heart]. The earnest (heartfelt, continued) prayer of a righteous man makes tremendous power available [dynamic in its working]" (James 5:16).

A Christian counselor's main goal should be to teach you to depend on God as soon as possible and not need further counseling. Some counselors teach ways to cope and treat symptoms. Others try to get at the root of the problem. Still others depend on God to root out the problem. The latter is the type of counselor to look for.

A counselor or dependable friend can coach you through difficulties and support you while you find your freedom. But no one can set you free, fix your problems, or heal you except God.

Confess your faults, but don't dump your responsibility onto others. We're responsible to let God heal us. Other people can encourage and love us, but they can't carry all our burdens for us.

When we were children, our parents were responsible for us. As adults, we're responsible for ourselves, and that includes our emotions. If we look for someone to take care of our emotions, we'll be disappointed. We can truly be free only when we cast our cares onto the Lord.

Look for a humble Christian friend or guide, someone who's on the same journey. We all have a lot to work on with God's help. Someone who acts superior will hurt you emotionally if he or she keeps you in a dependent, one-down position.

If God shows you that something is wrong, or if you have no peace about the relationship, then you may need to confront in love or say good-bye. God will lead you to safe friends and encouragers as you look to Him for guidance.

We need a boost from others to overcome chronic problems. If you recently lost a loved one, if you care for an invalid, or if you live with a difficult spouse, then you need support. Even if your emotions aren't severe enough to require professional help, you need encouragement from a mature Christian friend. A prayer partner will be a great help, even if you only pray over the phone once a week. If you find someone who's walking through a similar struggle, he or she will be thankful for your support as well.

Your spouse can be a great prayer partner even if your relationship isn't perfect. A key to successful partnership in prayer is trusting God to do what you can't. Faith in God's power to work through and in your relationship opens the door to miracles.

"Bear (endure, carry) one another's burdens and troublesome moral faults, and in this way fulfill and observe perfectly the law of Christ [the Messiah] and complete what is lacking [in your obedience to it]" (Gal. 6:2). But remember that God wants you to carry only a light burden. The key to staying free while counseling is to be aggressive about giving God the burdens of those you care for, along with your own.

Don't be too proud to ask for help, but be careful whom you ask. "Where no wise guidance is, the people fall, but in the multitude of counselors there is safety" (Prov. 11:14). As you look to Jesus for guidance, He'll bring faithful friends to encourage you along the way.

Checklist to Identify Areas of Unbelief in Relationships

1. Do you trust God with relationships at work? at church? with neighbors?
2. Do you trust God in social situations, or do you feel lost and alone?
3. Do you trust God when you argue with someone you love, or do you panic because you're afraid the relationship will end?
4. Do you believe God loves you enough to help you improve your relationships?
5. Do you suffer from jealousy and believe God loves others more than you?
6. Do you believe others care about you?
7. Are you unreasonably jealous of your spouse? Can you decide to trust God with this issue?
8. Do you have close friends you can trust with your heart's deepest struggles?

9. Do you have a mature friend or mentor to be accountable to?
10. Do you have a prayer partner?
11. Do you know someone in a similar situation? Could he or she become a safe friend to pray with?
12. Do you trust those whom God has placed in authority over you? If not, can you decide to trust God and ask Him to be in charge of those relationships?

Prayer of Trust for Relationships

Father, I praise You for Your love. Thank You for desiring above all else to be in loving relationship with me. I know You want me to love and be loved. I praise You for being all I need. Your love is more than I can contain.

Forgive me for having trouble trusting You with this relationship situation:

_____

_____

_____

_____

I choose to trust You now. I believe Your power can change things.

Even if others fail me, You'll always be there for me. I will trust You to bring more love into my life and to pour Your love through me to others. Teach me to trust You more. In Jesus' name. Amen.

11

Accept

A Divine Mediator

"Do not complain, brethren, against one another, so that you [yourselves] may not be judged. Look! The Judge is [already] standing at the very door" (James 5:9).

We cannot indulge in destructive actions or words, regardless of how we feel. It's wrong to dump anger onto others if we have a miserable day. We need to confess these attitudes to God and act in a loving way toward others even when we're sad, angry, afraid, or confused. If we pour emotional poison onto those we love, it can destroy our relationships and us.

Close relationships are the most challenging. If we allow God to transform our family and most intimate friendships, then His love will spill over to bless many.

Accept God's Presence and Wisdom in Relationships

Ask God for wisdom and direct intervention in every relationship. You may be a merciful person who wants to help others, but if it isn't God's idea, then you're on your own. If you don't listen to God when you try to help others, the consequences can be devastating. Yet God has power to bring good even out of bad circumstances when we turn to Him.

"Know this, that in the last days perilous times will come: For men will be lovers of themselves, lovers of money, boasters, proud, blasphemers, disobedient to parents, unthankful, unholy, unloving, unforgiving, slanderers, without self-control, brutal, despisers of good, traitors, headstrong, haughty, lovers of pleasure rather than lovers of God, having a form of godliness but denying its power. And from such people turn away! (2 Tim. 3:1-5, NKJV).

Accept God's direction as well as His love to be free of heavy burdens in your relationships. Emotional and spiritual dangers abound in this world. If a person is habitually damaging or his or her behavior fits into the above categories, it's wise to set boundaries with that person or turn away.

This doesn't mean God wants us to cut every annoying person out of our lives. It seems God usually blesses us with at least one difficult person: a child, spouse, sister, or boss. God can use these situations to teach us to love the unlovable. What could be more effective in revealing uncharitable feelings lurking in our hearts? So if you know God is teaching you through a hard relationship, take courage.

Who are the difficult people or situations that sandpaper your nerves, test your patience, and hurt your feelings? Thank God for them. They're God's most effective tools to chisel off your rough edges.

God allows us opportunities to learn to love the unlovable or to love through hard situations such as illness or handicaps. Nothing will grow us up quicker. Of course, it's crucial to cooperate, search for God's truth, and apply it. Applying scriptural principles, upholding honesty, speaking the truth in love, and forgiving enable us be joyful even in difficult circumstances.

The key is discerning whether God wants you to stay in a relationship or not. If you're confused about this, consult your pastor or a mature Christian. God leads us by peace. If you have no peace about a new relationship, it may not be God's will for you. When we want to befriend someone, if it's our idea and not God's, we may be in dangerous territory. Only God knows if there will be good results from that relationship or whether it will be unnecessarily burdensome. He may want us to spend our time elsewhere. Only God knows the best direction for the future.

Nothing good can result when we operate in the flesh. Whenever we act from our own thoughts, feelings, and reactions, we're operating in the flesh rather than the Spirit. This applies even when we think we're doing wonderful things for the Lord.

If we don't check with God and thus end up in an unwise relationship, we can't blame Him for the consequences.

"He who walks [as a companion] with wise men is wise, but he who associates with [self-confident] fools is [a fool himself and] shall smart for it" (Prov. 13:20).

As we invite God into each relationship, He'll give us specific wisdom to deal with each person and situation. He'll show us how to speak the truth in love and set healthful boundaries.

Set Loving Boundaries

"As iron sharpens iron, So a man sharpens the countenance of his friend" (Prov. 27:17, NKJV).

The proper motivation in setting boundaries is not only to protect ourselves but also to benefit the other person and protect the relationship.

One of the best keys to avoid accumulating heavy burdens is to set loving boundaries in relationships. It's wise to keep as many healthy relationships going as possible, but we need to keep people at different distances from our hearts. It's valuable to have many friendly acquaintances as well as a few close friends.

It's wise to go slowly in relationships. If you get close too soon, you may open yourself to unnecessary hurt. If you get to know people gradually, it should become obvious how trustworthy they'll be with your heart. Give others time to know you before opening your heart. You may lose a promising friendship if you dump burdens on them, especially at first. Don't swamp a developing friendship with a full history.

It's important to be able to recognize healthy relationships. If your friend tells you another friend's secrets, he or she probably won't keep your confidences either. Another criteria for whether a relationship is healthy or not is to notice if there are several positive interactions or comments for each negative one. It's not always easy to find emotionally trustworthy people. Some people may be safe only when kept at a certain distance.

Value friends who are safe enough to share your heart with—they're priceless treasures. It's wonderful to find friends we can be transparent with. You're blessed if you have even one safe, supportive friend who you can be accountable to with your deepest struggles.

We need to keep our eyes open to how people react in different situations. Some people are polite in group conversations but may be hurtfully critical one-on-one. Some parents may be very critical even when their child is an adult. In order to keep the best relationship possible, their son or daughter may decide to limit interactions with them.

It's not wise to expose yourself over and over again to harm. Why spend all your time trying to cope and heal emotionally? You have only so much time or energy. Why spend it on abusive people? There are so many better things to do.

Shutting someone out should be a rare occurrence, but if a person is a walking nightmare, use common sense and stay away. The only exception is if God gives you peace, support, and clear direction to reach out to that person.

Some people spend most of their lives trying to cope with one difficult person. God may use that relationship to transform them into the image of Christ and bring good from it. But if God is not directing them in that relationship, it won't be the best use of their time and energy.

Jesus said those who do God's will are his mother, sister, and brother. He felt as close to them as natural family. We have no choice about the family we're born into. However, as we get older, we do have choices. We have choices in the situations and amounts of time we spend with friends and family. We can choose to spend the most time with those who uplift us and draw us closer to the Father.

Focus on positives in relationships, but be aware of negatives. Often we can set boundaries on unhealthful aspects but keep the positive parts of our relationships. Ask God for wisdom in each relationship.

Jesus reached out to everyone in ministry. He loved everyone, but he did not entrust himself to just anyone. "Jesus [for His part] did not trust Himself to them, because He knew all [men]; And He did not need anyone to bear witness concerning man [needed no evidence from anyone about men], for He Himself knew what was in human nature. [He could read men's hearts.]" (John 2:24-25).

Speaking the truth in love (Eph. 4:15) is key to healthy relationships. It's important to communicate with our family and friends and let them know if they hurt our feelings. Healthy relationships have healthful boundaries. Just as boundary lines keep peace between neighbors, so boundaries can keep peace in relationships. Healthy love is a balance of nurturing and setting reasonable boundaries with others. We can discipline children and set boundaries with family and friends in loving ways.

People usually won't listen if our attitudes or tone of voice is harsh. They can tell if we carry a burden of anger, because it spills out through body language and tone of voice. However, if we let go of our anger and forgive, they'll feel that too. If we love others, they'll be more open to what we say.

We also need boundaries so we can heal. If someone hit you with a bat every time you got close, you would probably keep your distance. In fact, your friends would say you would be crazy to get near that person. However, often we don't pay any attention to emotional abuse, or we tell ourselves that we're too sensitive.

Loving our neighbor does not mean we should enable him or her to be destructive. We encourage hurtful behavior if we let someone into our home when we know he or she will steal from us or when we excuse someone who's abusive. Making it easy for others to engage in negative behavior is not love—it's enabling evil to fester in their lives and infect others. But when we confront or oppose them, God wants us to do it in love.

Love means we don't shut people out unless no other good choice exists. But tough love can sometimes turn around a difficult relationship with a rebellious teen or a difficult adult. The message should be "I love and forgive you, but I will not support your destructive behavior. The door will be open if you have a change of heart and actions."

Of course, it's important to forgive. But it's wise to protect yourself in reasonable ways so you have less hurt to forgive. We can be as "wary and wise as serpents, and be innocent (harmless, guileless, and without falsity) as doves" (Matt. 10:16).

Jesus spoke about forgiving "seventy times seven," and "turning the other cheek," but this must be balanced with verses such as 2 Tim. 3:5, which advises us to stay away from evil, unloving people. Prov. 27:5-6 tells us, "Open rebuke is better than love that is hidden. Faithful are the wounds of a friend, but the kisses of an enemy are lavish and deceitful." 1 Cor. 5:9-13 also speaks of disciplining and avoiding those who cause severe problems.

All healthy relationships need boundaries. Others won't know how we feel unless we tell them. Fences make good neighbors. We'll have a better relationship if our fence keeps their children from trampling our garden.

Verbal and emotional abuse can be just as damaging as physical abuse. If someone yells at us, calls us names, or talks to us in a harsh tone it can wound and burden our hearts. If they disappoint us constantly, that can become a burden to us as well.

Emotional abuse is sometimes more damaging than physical abuse, because it's often left untreated and unhealed. We may not think it's important, because we can't see emotional wounds. We need to protect ourselves from verbally abusive people just as we would protect ourselves from physical harm. But we need to do it in love.

If you're bound to an abusive person by marriage or a job, the best strategy is still to protect yourself as much as possible. Difficult relationships need radical, truthful, aggressive forgiveness, to work through it with God's help. The only way to be happy in any relationship is to decide to always forgive and trust God again with the situation. As you heal, God will help you to brush off unkind words more easily, before they burden you.

Don't deny emotions. If you're hurt, angry, or even full of rage, the remedy starts with complete honesty with your own soul and with God. Pour it all out to the Father, just as King David did in the Psalms. He vented his emotions to God in ways that often don't sound very spiritual. He brought all the unrest of his soul first to God and put his trust in God for the problem.

After we get the poison out of our system, we can trust that God will forgive and grant wisdom to handle the situation. We can confront others in love. However, this is usually much more effective after the force of the emotion has calmed down. We should not confront anyone unless we have peace from God to proceed.

Confronting should always be done in love. We need to wait

until we care about the other person. Timing is important. It's difficult to care about the person who hurt you until you're healed by God's love.

Get out of any relationships prohibited by God's Word, even if they seem positive. God doesn't want you in unhealthy, damaging relationships. If you're in a sinful relationship, end or correct it to fit into God's guidelines to prevent painful consequences.

God will give peace beyond our understanding even in difficult circumstances if we're in His will. Suffering has value only if it's according to the will of God. It's stupid to suffer in relationships of our own choosing.

If your relationship is within God's guidelines and you know God wants you to be in that relationship, then trust God to change the situation. You should be the one to start being more positive by God's grace. Your improved attitude should eventually rub off on the other person. If you wait for the other person to change first, it probably will never happen.

God can bless you in spite of emotionally abusive or neglectful people in your life if you trust Him and focus on Him in faith and not on the person who's hurting you. But don't be in denial. Bring God's truth into your circumstances—don't just hope problems will go away. Aggressive confession of our own negative emotions and thoughts, ongoing forgiveness, and a decision to love by God's grace are the only ways to be happy in close relationships.

Invite God to be in charge, trust in Him, and don't worry. God will shine light and love into your relationship, and you'll probably see the other person start to change. When God's Spirit works in you, it's contagious.

We're not responsible for others' behavior, but we *are* responsible for our *own* attitudes, words, and actions. Regardless of how others treat us, whether they're kind or abusive, we're still responsible before God to respond in the right way.

If you're unhappy in a relationship, ask God for specific directions. Does He want you to let go of and grieve the relationship? Or does He want you to grow stronger to overcome the relationship obstacles?

It starts with admitting any attitudes of frustration, discouragement, boredom, bitterness, or resentment. God starts with us, not the other person.

God values love and relationships. He wants to heal the hurts and blocks within you that keep you from forming close relationships. Open up all your loneliness and hurt to God. Place your trust in Him. God wants you to be loved. He'll heal you and bring positive Christian relationships into your life.

Avoid Unnecessary Relationship Burdens

The easiest way to stay free of burdens is to avoid taking them on in the first place. Unless we know God wants us to be involved in a burdensome situation, it's smart to avoid it. God gave us common sense so we would use it.

We only have so much strength and energy to deal with heavy situations. It makes no sense to take on more than we can handle. We need to be realistic about our limitations. If we help so many people that we become overwhelmed and start sinking emotionally, we aren't wise managers. If we loan out so much money that we become bankrupt, is that wisdom? If we give out until we're emotionally bankrupt, what good is that?

The key is to ask God in every situation whether it's His will that we be involved in it or not. Sometimes we can see a need and think, *Of course, it would be God's will for me to help*. But this is not always true. When it's our own idea to get involved in some good work, often we're leaning on our own understanding and are not in God's will. Although I believe He understands our good intentions, we still may continually struggle, because God is trying to tell us we're in the wrong place.

We can't help others if we're going under. We have to let Jesus carry most of the weight. If we continually struggle with a relationship, we need to specifically ask God if He wants us involved. Perhaps He does want us to help, but we need to set up loving boundaries. Ask God for wisdom.

When we start being aware of burdens, it's easy to see how people can quickly become weighed down. We can learn to handle relationships so we avoid being unnecessarily burdened. Over time we can also develop more resistance to being hurt. We can learn to accept helpful feedback but reject harsh criticism or condemnation, letting the unwise words of others fall off our rain-coat of God's grace. We can learn to focus on the good in relationships and trust God to take care of the problems.

God will forgive us for not trusting Him in the past and give us relief from heavy loads. As we step out on faith, accept Jesus into each problem, and trust His power to rescue us, we find freedom.

When we wait upon God for step-by-step direction in relationships and stop relying on our own judgment, we'll avoid taking on unwise burdens. When we protect our relationships, shine God's love on them, and water relationships with kindness, goodness will grow. Relationships don't need to be difficult. If we focus on the positive, trust God, and accept His help, love will flower.

Checklist to Accept God's Help for Your Relationships

1. Do you have relationships you never asked God to be in charge of?
2. What's stopping you?
3. Do you consult God before forming new relationships or trying to help others?
4. Have you invited Jesus into your neighborhood, work, and church relationships?
5. Do you ask God to take over when you run into a snag with these people?
6. Are you willing to expose your closest relationships to the light of God's love and truth?
7. Are you willing to allow God to enable you to continually forgive everyone?
8. Are you willing to love others by God's grace, even when they don't deserve it?
9. Are you willing to trust God enough to guide you to correct or release unhealthy relationships?
10. Is there a chronic difficulty in a relationship you never invited Jesus to rescue you from?
11. Has it always been hard to trust God to change that situation?
12. Are you willing to step out in faith and decide to trust Him now? If not, talk to God about it. Admit you have trouble

trusting, ask Him to forgive you for not believing Him, and ask Him to help you trust Him so you can accept His help.

Prayer for Healthy Relationships

Father, I praise You for loving me more than I can imagine. I believe You want me to have healthy relationships. I trust that You have my best interest at heart and that You'll guide me in each relationship.

Thank You for inventing relationships. All love finds its source in You. I invite You into the heart of my relationships. I ask You to direct my thoughts, attitudes, words, and actions toward others. I admit that I can't handle my relationships on my own. I pray for Your Spirit to wash over all my relationships with healing water and oil of Your Spirit. Remove the rough spots.

For any difficult relationship You want me to be committed to, I pray for patience and love. I open up to You all the areas of hurt and anger in my heart. I confess that I tried to handle things on my own and didn't completely trust You. I ask and believe that You'll forgive and heal me. By Your grace, I choose to forgive all those who have hurt me for every past, present, and future hurt. I choose to walk in the freedom of forgiveness. Pour Your love through me, and let me feel Your joy.

I lift up every relationship in complete trust to You. I put You totally in charge; tell me what to do each step of the way. I choose to give up any relationships that are not Your will for me. I will do my best to listen, obey, and not lean on my own understanding. I ask You to invade all my relationships and bring Your peace, joy, wisdom, and healing power. I lean on and totally rely on You. I bring You all my feelings, thoughts, and actions for Your cleansing, healing, and guidance. I believe Jesus is the Son of God and that He died to forgive my sins and set me free so I can have an abundant life, including healthy relationships. I accept Jesus as my Savior in all areas of my life and relationships. In His name I pray. Amen.

12
Faith in Action
Love Restored

═══════════◎═══════════

"Two are better than one, because they have a good [more satisfying] reward for their labor; For if they fall, the one will lift up his fellow. But woe to him who is alone when he falls and has not another to lift him up! And though a man might prevail against him who is alone, two will withstand him. A threefold cord is not quickly broken" (Eccles. 4:9-10, 12).

Love is restored when relationships are freed from heavy burdens. As you're freed emotionally, the next step toward an abundant life is to let God's love, forgiveness, and mercy flow through you to touch others. Emotional freedom is not found in perpetual self-examination. Reaching out and bringing joy to others, as God leads, makes life worth living.

When we give from the heart, God's Holy Spirit carries us and sets us free. Giving from an attitude of faith, peace, and love brings joy. Giving from a motive of guilt or fear of what others think brings misery and increases burdens. Let the love of God flow through you, not fear of people. We experience true joy by allowing God's abundant love to flow through us.

Right now we have two Islamic women from Afghanistan staying with us. Even though their schedule is demanding, we drive them back and forth to school and around town. They've brought much joy into our lives, and we'll miss them when they return to Kabul. God knits hearts together within His masterpiece of life, often in ways we could never predict.

We can trust God to protect us as we continue to love, forgive, and give to others. God wants His love to surge in torrents through the cleansed vessels of our lives to heal a hurting world. God's love can't be contained. The nature of life, love, and joy is expansion, growth, and generosity. Life is messy and impossible to box in. But as we give joy away every day, we'll be renewed and will enliven everyone we touch with God's love.

In our quest to become free, we must keep a balance. Yes, you can find peace through confessing heart truths, trusting God, and releasing burdens as you accept God's help. You can keep your peace through limiting negative exposure, setting healthful boundaries, and exercising wisdom.

Don't go overboard protecting yourself to the extent that you become self-absorbed. Reach out to others, and allow your life to be disrupted to some extent. Otherwise, you'll be stifled and bored. Wrapping life into efficient packages does not allow for the priceless serendipities that bring us joy. Life, love, and joy can't flourish in neat, little boxes.

Loving others can be exhilarating, inconvenient, or even exhausting. But remember—anything orchestrated by God's love will fit into His master plan and bring overwhelming joy.

A Completely New Life

Stephanie was a Christian woman in her 60s. She had suffered from mild depression for as long as she could remember. She didn't feel loved by her parents or her first husband, and she was estranged from her grown children.

Stephanie married again, this time to a younger man. They came to see me for marriage counseling. The main problem was her bitter attitude.

Stephanie loved the Lord. When she understood there was a way out of her misery, she was excited and became committed to the process of letting God carry her through doors of pain and releasing her burdens. She became radically honest with God, confessed her burdens of hurt and bitterness, believed in Jesus' power to deliver her, and accepted Him into every heart-wound God revealed to her.

Each of Stephanie's relationships improved as she learned to forgive from her heart. At the end of counseling, her husband told me she was "a completely different person." The couple then began to minister to others in their church.

Deliverance from Lifelong Patterns

Bonnie was a Christian who had been struggling with out-of-control anger for years. She was too harsh with her children and with herself. Her mother had been verbally and physically abusive, and Bonnie was shocked to see the same emotional patterns within herself. I asked her to journal her feelings.

The next time we met I asked if she was able to get some journaling done. She said, "No, I haven't, because every time I try to write out what my anger would say, all I can think of are swear words."

I told her the anger within her needed to be cleaned out. If she felt like swearing, she needed to admit it to God. God already knew everything within her heart.

She was able to journal after that. Bonnie confessed, and she invited Jesus to rescue her from these attitudes. At the end of counseling, she had victory over her anger problems. Bonnie told me she never experienced such peace before, or such love for her children. Parenting, with more love and less anger, was a wonderful new experience.

Developing a Support Network

Teresa was back in my office again. It had been nearly a year since I had seen her. She wore her hair in a different, softer style.

"How are you doing, Teresa?"

"Actually I'm doing pretty well. I have a Bible study I go to every week. I have more positive friendships. I get together with friends from my church much more often than I used to. Today I'm just wondering how to set some boundaries with my roommate."

Teresa was a never-married, 35-year-old when I first met her. She had few friends and felt insecure in those friendships. She grew up with parents who cared but didn't know how to communicate love. She had felt lonely all her life. But now her relationship network was growing, and Teresa carried herself with more confidence.

Excruciating loneliness is common in our society. Several factors are involved. People keep a frantic pace, and many are overwhelmed with work and family demands. Too tired to socialize after work, they collapse in front of the television set or log on to the Internet. Some have added complications such as a difficult teen or dependent parents.

It takes time to find and develop deep friendships. Children and teens have time to bond with friends. Working adults and those with families have limited time and often don't have energy to invest in making new friends. Some are fortunate enough to keep close friends from childhood, but many others are transplanted and must start over. If you recently moved, this is the reality to overcome to develop a network of friends. For most of us (except super extroverts), this can be difficult.

God wants us to love and be loved. He wants us to have good friends and to stay as close to our families as possible. He'll give us creative wisdom to find time and ways to form healthy relationships. He wants us to have friends close enough to be like mothers, fathers, brothers, and sisters.

In order to accept love from God or others, we must open our hearts. How can others truly know or love you if you hide your feelings? If you're too ashamed to let anyone close, you'll always feel lonely. No one will be able to touch you in the depths of your heart if your heart doors are shut.

A good strategy for developing a network of supportive friends is to use every opportunity to interact with others as you ask God for guidance. Focus on the positive in everyone you meet. As you experience God's love more, you can pass it on to others. Start with showing interest by listening to and encouraging others. Ask questions, and focus more on others than on yourself.

If you encounter people who are negative or seem to reject you, throw that burden onto the Lord's shoulders as quickly as possible, and move on. Don't mourn the loss of a cup of cold water when you have a faucet connected to a limitless supply. God is more than able to fill your lonely spaces.

Invite people you're comfortable with to lunch or to your home. Choose wisely; invite only friendly, positive people who seem interested. Keep asking different people one after another. Be creative. Invite one person or a couple for coffee, and the next week invite someone else to an event. When you run into friends, take some time to talk, or grab the opportunity to go out for coffee.

Don't focus on just one relationship. Even those interested in friendship may be too busy. If too many things interfere with getting together with them, let go and pursue other friendships. Enjoy their company, seek to bless them, and don't expect anything in return. At the end of your conversation, ask if there's anything they would like you to pray about, and then pray for them. Eventually some will reciprocate, and you'll be able to develop lots of friendly acquaintances and a few close confidants.

Many clients have used this strategy and found it helpful. However, we must admit our helplessness, depend on God, and invite Jesus into the middle of all our relationships. If we don't, even our best-laid plans may fail.

God created us to be social, interdependent beings. We're healthiest when we're loved. We all need friends and support on many levels.

Walk in Peace, Love, and Joy

The only way to walk in peace, love, and joy is to walk in the Spirit. These desirable emotions are fruits of God's Spirit, not ours. They won't be present in our lives unless we're filled with His Spirit. If we're guided by the Spirit's peace and motivated by God's love, joy will result.

"That which is desired in a man is loyalty and kindness [and his glory and delight are his giving]" (Prov. 19:22).

We can't be truly joyful without learning to love and give to others. It's impossible to continue to love someone unless we continue to forgive. As we receive God's love and forgiveness, we must love and forgive others in order to stay free.

God forgives the unforgivable and can enable us to do the same. Make it your goal to release burdens others place on you as quickly as possible. Make a decision to forgive any difficult person God has placed in your life for all past, present, and future problems they cause you. You'll still have to release new burdens, but when your decision to always forgive is in place, it becomes much easier. Bitterness is a heavy burden. Forgiveness sets us free.

"And the harvest of righteousness (of conformity to God's will in thought and deed) is [the fruit of the seed] sown in peace by those who work for and make peace [in themselves and in others, that peace which means concord, agreement, and harmony between individuals, with undisturbedness, in a peaceful mind free from fears and agitating passions and moral conflicts]" (James 3:18).

"Mark the blameless man and behold the upright, for there is a happy end for the man of peace" (Ps. 37:37).

One of the most valuable lessons God has taught me in ministering to others is never to help anyone or do anything I don't have peace about. One of my spiritual gifts is mercy, but trying to help people because I thought it was a good idea instead of checking first with God caused me some unnecessary trouble in the past. If your spiritual gift is mercy also, be careful about this. Don't do something you don't have peace about. Following God's peace keeps us free emotionally.

"Peace I leave with you; my peace I give you. I do not give to you as the world gives. Do not let your hearts be troubled and do not be afraid" (John 14:27, NIV).

Staying Free Requires Obedience

"If you abide in My Word [hold fast to My teachings and live in accordance with them], you are truly My disciples. And you will know the Truth, and the Truth will set you free" (John 8:31-32).

"[Live] as free people, [yet] without employing your freedom as a pretext for wickedness; but [live at all times] as servants of God" (1 Pet. 2:16).

We achieve stability as we become free by obeying God's Word and pacing ourselves. We can't successfully navigate life's stormy waters without a firm faith in God and a trust in His Guidebook, the Bible. Read or meditate on His Word regularly—not to fulfill some self-righteous rules but to be fed spiritual nourishment that gives strength to go on.

"Blessed (Happy, fortunate, prosperous, and enviable) is the man who walks and lives not in the counsel of the ungodly [following their advice, their plans and purposes], nor stands [submissive and inactive] in the path where sinners walk, nor sits down [to relax and rest] where the scornful [and the mockers] gather. But his delight and desire are in the law of the Lord, and on His law (the precepts, the instructions, the teachings of God) he habitually meditates (ponders and studies) by day and by night. And he shall be like a tree firmly planted [and tended] by the streams of water, ready to bring forth its fruit in its season; its leaf also shall not fade or wither; and everything he does shall prosper [and come to maturity]" (Ps. 1:1-3).

Obeying God's laws doesn't inhibit us—it actually frees us to be what God created us to be. When we avoid sin, we also avoid burdens of guilt and damage from unwise choices. "I run in the path of your commands, for you have set my heart free" (Ps. 119:32, NIV).

Staying Free Requires Humility

"Blessed (happy, to be envied, and spiritually prosperous—with life-joy and satisfaction in God's favor and salvation, regardless of their outward conditions) are the poor in spirit (the humble, rating themselves insignificant), for theirs is the kingdom of heaven!" (Matt. 5:3).

We will be motivated to spend time with God when we're humble enough to realize how desperately we need Him. Quiet times with God help us remain emotionally free. These times with the Lord provide the quiet and rest that we need. Often we become burdened because we keep ourselves so busy that we don't pay attention to our emotions and deal with them regularly.

Emotional freedom is found on a humble path. When we realize that in ourselves we can do no good thing (see Rom. 7:18), this actually sets us free from burdens. Why worry about something we're not capable of correcting in our own strength? No one really likes to admit helplessness. But when we're humbled by realizing our helplessness, we're in the best place to break through to more freedom.

We can't walk in freedom in our own strength. God does it for us. "In Him we live and move and have our being" (Acts 17:28). Apart from God we can't even live or breathe, let alone do anything else. It may appear we're accomplishing a lot, but if God isn't in it, our efforts are worthless.

As we lean totally upon the Lord, we can do all things through Him who strengthens us (Phil. 4:13). Freedom is found by resting in God's sufficiency rather than struggling to get free. "There remains therefore a rest for the people of God. For he who has entered His rest has himself also ceased from his works as God did from His. Let us therefore be diligent to enter that rest, lest anyone fall according to the same example of disobedience" (Heb. 4:9-11, NKJV).

How can we find rest for our souls? What does it mean to cease from our own works? We can rest in knowing that we don't have to rely on our own strength. We can't succeed or attain emotional freedom by our own efforts. But God will grant miracles of grace as we trust and bring everything to Him. Once we stop struggling and striving, God explodes onto the scene. It's about letting Him work and getting out of His way.

We all know Christians who walk in freedom. Billy Graham and others like him are heroes of our faith. Humility and giving all the glory to God are keys to their freedom. Christians who have been used mightily by God tell us that they can take none of the credit, that it's God who makes great things happen.

It isn't enough to simply ask God for His help. We must give Him complete control of every facet of our days. When we try in our strength, we get in God's way, and we end up carrying our own burdens again. God can't take them for us, because we're handling them ourselves. Every morning admit that you're not able to carry the burdens of the day. Ask God to forgive you for trying instead of trusting.

As we continue to release heavy burdens, we become aware that it's easier not to shoulder them in the first place. Christ must live through us and be in control if we want to be free and to rest in God. Every day we can place our burdens and concerns into His capable hands. Then we can walk in freedom, as little children, trusting our Heavenly Father to control our lives. We find freedom in humility.

"In [this] freedom Christ has made us free [and completely liberated us]; stand fast then, and do not be hampered and held ensnared and submit again to a yoke of slavery [which you have once put off]" (Gal. 5:1).

Life Abundant

"Save your people and bless your inheritance; be their shepherd and carry them forever" (Ps. 28:9, NIV).

The only way to life abundant is to rest in God's arms and never let go of faith in Him. As God's truth, grace, and love flush the poison from our hearts, then His life and light flow through our spiritual and emotional veins. Health, wealth, and social standing are not necessarily indications of an abundant life. True abundance depends on God's presence and letting His life, love, and joy flow through you.

The abundant life is not a destination where life suddenly becomes perfect upon our arrival. Rather, it's more like a successful war or a difficult but victorious journey.

This myth of the perfect abundant life makes many people miserable. They think, *If only I would pray more, read the Bible more, or give more—then God would be happy with me, and everything will be perfect.* Wrong. The only perfect place is heaven.

Even after the Israelites entered their promised land, they still faced many battles ahead. But as they trusted God, He carried them to victory. Abundant life is being carried by the everlasting, all-powerful, forever-loving God through and over all of life's challenges.

If the apostle Paul could experience contentment and abundant life in spite of prison and persecution, then you can too. Right now, in spite of your circumstances, you can experience this. If Jesus is your Lord, if you love God and do your best to live for Him, then God is happy with you now. It doesn't matter if your roof leaks, your bank account is empty, your daughter is angry with you, and you're not popular—you can rejoice in God's love now.

"Who shall ever separate us from Christ's love? Shall suffering and affliction and tribulation? Or calamity and distress? Or persecution or hunger or destitution or peril or sword? . . .

"Amid all these things we are more than conquerors and gain a surpassing victory through Him Who loved us. For I am persuaded beyond doubt (am sure) that neither death nor life, nor angels nor principalities, nor things impending and threatening, nor things to come, nor powers, Nor height nor depth, nor anything else in all creation will be able to separate us from the love of God which is in Christ Jesus our Lord" (Rom. 8:35, 37-39).

An abundant life promises a rich heart and contentment. It may include physical blessings, such as money and great health, but not always. It's a place of rest in God and richness within the spirit that doesn't always make sense if you look at circumstances. Life abundant is joy in spite of sorrow, hope in the face of despair, love that overcomes, and faith that wins the victory.

A person may have only enough money to meet his or her needs but be wealthy in terms of loving relationships and peace with God. A good example is the classic movie *It's a Wonderful Life*. I'm not sure that every time a bell rings an angel gets his or her wings, but I'm sure God wants us to have a meaningful, abundant life.

Jesus said, "The thief comes only in order to steal and kill and destroy. I came that they may have and enjoy life, and have it in abundance (to the full, till it overflows)" (John 10:10).

God placed seeds of vast potential within our hearts. As the burdens (the poisonous sludge of painful emotions) are removed and God's power flows through our lives, these seeds have a chance to grow. When we're weighed down and stifled by burdens, we lose potential for growth. God can cleanse and mend our hearts so that we can function and flourish as He originally intended.

Jesus said, "I am the Vine; you are the branches. Whoever lives in Me and I in him bears much (abundant) fruit. However, apart from Me [cut off from vital union with Me] you can do nothing. . . . If you live in Me [abide vitally connected to Me] and My words remain in you and continue to live in your hearts, ask whatever you will, and it shall be done for you. . . . I have told you these things, that My joy and delight may be in you, and that your joy and gladness may be full measure and complete and overflowing" (John 15:5, 7, 11).

We are never the source of our own joy. Jesus is our source, and we experience the abundant life only as we live in vital union with Him. As we humbly allow Him free reign over every area of our hearts and emotions, the abundance of our lives grows.

God is anxious to give us the resources we need to experience fruitful lives. As we stay free from burdens and stay connected to

Him, the fruit of His Spirit will grow, and we'll experience more love, joy, peace, patience, kindness, goodness, faithfulness, gentleness, and self-control (Gal. 5:22).

As we grow strong in the Lord, we outgrow many problems. We may still have difficulties, but they don't keep us down. We become more stable and can withstand more pressure. A blow to a sapling can easily damage it, but it's difficult to hurt a full-grown oak tree.

". . . they may be called oaks of righteousness [lofty, strong and magnificent, distinguished for uprightness, justice, and right standing with God], the planting of the Lord, that He may be glorified" (Isa. 61:3).

As Sarah's heart healed, her kindness grew toward her family and herself. Her courage increased as she realized that it was safe to make mistakes in her journey with God. Her sessions became much lighter; sometimes we laughed together about her daughter's exploits. She learned to bring burdens to God on her own and ran out of problems to talk about in our sessions. We ended therapy, but Sarah said she would return if she got stuck. I told her my door was always open.

I pray that you'll also find rest in God's arms. Every morning ask God to carry you through—and you'll soar on freedom's wings.

Checklist to Stay Free and Continually Accept God's Help

1. Are you expecting God to act in the same ways all the time? Are you missing the new thing He's trying to do in your life?
2. Do you focus more on positives or negatives?
3. Are you willing to ask God to enable you to focus more on the good in your life and relationships?
4. What have you done for fun this week with friends and family?
5. Do you consider yourself better than anyone, or do you realize that we're all dependent on God's grace and generosity?
6. Do your relationships lift you up or burden you? Have you sought God's wisdom for each relationship?
7. Have you spent time in God's Word and prayed recently?
8. Is there anyone you need to forgive?

9. Is there a burden you can release to God today?
10. Is there a relationship you can invite Jesus into?
11. Do you realize that nothing is impossible for God?
12. Do you feel more of God's incomprehensible, amazing, all-encompassing love for you?

Morning Prayer

Lord, I praise You for Your overwhelming power to set me free. You know the future; You know the path to freedom. I confess that I can't direct my own way. Reveal Your good will for my life as I humbly submit to You. By Your grace, show me how to be responsible for my own emotions and not to dump them onto others.

You have compassion on all my wounds, physical and emotional. I thank You that I can trust You with all I am and all I feel. Give me the courage to bring everything about myself into the light of Your truth. As I open my heart, remove the pain. I put all my trust in You. Forgive me for trying so hard to cope with burdens on my own. Give me wisdom to see the emotional burdens I carry. Help me to release them all, one by one, into Your care. Thank You so much for being willing to carry my burdens for me.

You're more than able to handle anything I'll face today. I release all my cares to You. All my concerns, burdens, obligations, and relationships I put into Your hands. I won't worry, because I trust You. I place You in total control of my life. I will obey You. Let me be who You created me to be. Lead me in the path of wisdom and life.

Jesus, bring Your light, love, and healing power into my dark, lonely emotions. Let Your love overflow from my heart to bless others. Thank You that it's Your desire to set me free. I thank You in advance for the good You'll accomplish through my life.

I believe it's Your desire to give me abundant life right now by faith. Fill my heart, soul, and spirit with Your life, love, and joy. Lift me on wings of hope to soar above my circumstances. In the miracle-working name of Jesus I pray. Amen.

"I will give them a heart to know me, that I am the LORD. They will be my people, and I will be their God, for they will return to me with all their heart" (Jer. 24:7).

Notes

Chapter 1

1. *American Heritage Dictionary of the English Language, New College Edition*, s.v. "motion," s.v. "emotion."

2. Ibid., s.v. "heart."

3. My appreciation to John Marquez for relating this to me.

Chapter 2

1. *Al-Anon's Twelve Steps & Twelve Traditions* (Virginia Beach, Va.: Al-Anon Family Group Headquarters, 1981), 3.

2. Quoted in Rick Warren, *The Purpose-Driven Life* (Grand Rapids: Zondervan Publishing House, 2002), 79.

3. *Strong's Exhaustive Concordance of the Bible*, (McLean, Va.: MacDonald Publishing Co., n.d.), s.v. "salvation."

4. *Smith's Bible Dictionary*, comp. William Smith (Nashville: Thomas Nelson Publishers, 1986), s.v. "angels."

Chapter 4

1. My appreciation to my dad, Pastor Al Runge, for his verbal testimony.

Chapter 7

1. *American Heritage Dictionary*, s.v. "justified."

Chapter 8

1. *Strong's Exhaustive Concordance of the Bible*, s.v. "mind."

Chapter 9

1. *The Medical Works of Hippocrates* (London: A. R. Mowbray & Co. Limited, 1950), 35.

Recommended Reading

The Lord and His Levite
John Marquez
(available through Christlifesolutions.org)

31 Days of Praise
Ruth Myers

Pilgrim's Progress
John Bunyan

Bondage Breaker
Neil Anderson

Boundaries
John Townsend

Telling Yourself the Truth
William Backus
Marie Chapian

Forgive and Forget
Lewis Smedes

A Brooklyn Jew Meets Jesus
Pastor Albert Runge

Humility
Andrew Murray

The Power of a Praying Woman
Stormie Omartian

For more helpful resources, visit
www.RobinMartens.com